Fisher Press

NICHOLAS WISEMAN

Nicholas Wiseman was born in 1802 in Seville where his father was a merchant. Both sides of his family had their roots in Ireland. While an infant his mother consecrated him to the service of the Church in Seville Cathedral. After his father's early death his mother returned to Ireland, but she sent him at the age of 8 to board in England at Ushaw College in Co. Durham. Here he was treated with favour by Dr. Lingard, the Vice Rector, who was already researching for his magisterial *History of England*.

At the age of 16 he was one of the small party of students sent to Rome to study at the Venerable English College after its restoration by Pius VII. He gained his Doctorate after the usual public disputation, and because of his high linguistic and scholastic abilities won an open competition for the post of Professor of Oriental Languages at the University of Rome. He was frequently received by Pius VII, and at the age of 26 was appointed Rector of the English College. His hugely popular lectures in London in 1835 and 1836 on the Catholic Faith, given largely to Protestant audiences, brought him national fame. In 1850 he was made a Cardinal and chosen by Pius IX to restore the ecclesiastical hierarchy in England. When he took up office Catholics were still largely a persecuted sect; by the time of his death in 1865 they had come to be accepted as members of a Church which was playing an increasingly significant role in national life.

Despite his episcopal duties Cardinal Wiseman continued to pursue his scholarly and artistic interests. In 1854 he published a successful novel, *Fabiola*, about early Christians in Rome, and in 1858 his *Recollections of the Last Four Popes and of Rome in their Times*.

Published by Fisher Press, Post Office Box 41,
Sevenoaks, Kent TN15 6YN, England

Pius VII was first published in 1858 as part of
Nicholas Wiseman's
*Recollections of the Last Four Popes
and of Rome in their Times*

First published as a Fisher paperback 2003

All rights reserved
Cover picture: © Tate, London, 2003

No part of this publication may be reproduced, stored in a
retrieval system, or transmitted, in any form or by any
means, electronic, mechanical, photocopying, recording or
otherwise, without the prior permission of Fisher Press.

This book is sold subject to the condition that it shall not,
by way of trade or otherwise, be lent, re-sold, hired out or
otherwise circulated without the publisher's prior consent
in any form of binding or cover other than in which it is
published and without a similar condition being imposed
on the subsequent purchaser.

British Library Cataloguing in Publication Data

A catalogue record for this book is available from
The British Library

ISBN 1 874037 17 5

Printed by Antony Rowe (Eastbourne) Ltd

NICHOLAS WISEMAN

PIUS
THE SEVENTH

Fisher Press

i

INTRODUCTION

A T a time when many are disillusioned with their temporal and even some of their spiritual leaders, it is tempting for Christians to adopt the lazy unhistorical views of the cynics around them. These claim that wise and disinterested leadership is impossible. Christians may defend their adoption of this theologically unsound position by claiming that self-seeking in a leader is to be expected in the light of original sin. But this is to ignore the possibility of grace and the workings of Providence, which a close scrutiny of history will reveal.

Cardinal Wiseman's portrait of Pius VII and of the spirit of Rome during his papacy, forms the first part of his *Recollections of the last Four Popes and of Life in Rome in their Times*. It is a compelling refutation of the cynic's case. Despite being without great intellectual gifts, and having spent his formative years as a Benedictine monk in retirement from the world of secular and clerical politics, Barnabas Chiaramonti, when called to the Church's highest office, was able to govern the Church and Papal States in very difficult times with considerable effectiveness. He did this because at a human level he had the gift of choosing ministers and advisers of outstanding talent, and because, as a transparently good and holy man, he was able to inspire others with unflinching personal loyalty to himself. But he also had a clear sense of what was in the interests of the Church and of his temporal domain, and a trust in Divine Providence, which he combined with the virtues of both prudence and fortitude.

The contrast between Pius VII and Wiseman is striking: in intellect, character and fortune. Wiseman was intellectually brilliant and urbane and, unlike Barnabas Chiaramonti, success came to him early: he rose, almost without a single setback, to become the first Archbishop of Westminster.

Wiseman, who was born in 1802, was top of his class at Ushaw College; he received his Doctorate of Divinity after a public disputation in Rome before a group of international scholars before he had reached the age of 22. He was a priest of the Catholic Church at 23. In 1827 he gained an international reputation with the publication of his *Horae Syriacae*. This was a scholarly philological contribution to the study of the Syriac versions of the Old Testament made through his work on the "Karkaphensian Codex" in the Vatican Library. With this success, and after a public competition, he was appointed Professor of Oriental Languages at the University of Rome by Leo XII. Wiseman was already fluent in Spanish, French, Italian and Arabic. In 1828, when he was 26, he was appointed Rector of the English College.

As Rector Wiseman was now someone whom many Englishmen, both Protestants and Catholic, came to see when visiting the Eternal City. In the absence of diplomatic relations the College must have had something of the flavour of a small British legation in a major European city. With his languages, his urbanity and his wide culture—so wide that some critics spoke of him as a *dilettante*,—what an international figure he must have seemed to visitors from England emerging from the isolation of the Napoleonic period, and how formidable. Newman and Hurrell Froude called on him in 1833. According to Froude, Wiseman made it clear that on the subject of their relations with Rome "not one step could be taken without swallowing the Council of Trent whole."

In the mid 1830s Wiseman's attention began to turn more and more towards England. In 1835 and 1836 he gave a series of sensational lectures in London at the Sardinian Chapel and at St Mary Moorfields. He lecturerd in the evening to vast crowds, most of them Protestants. Because of the crush many stood for the almost two hours that the lectures lasted. The topic of each lecture was some aspect of the universal doctrines of the Catholic Church: the real presence, transubstantiation, indulgences, the supremacy of the Pope, and the Protestant and Catholic attitudes to Faith. This was the first time since the expulsion of James II that the London public was able, in large numbers, to gather and listen to the truths of the Catholic Faith being expounded clearly and with intellectual coherence by a person of high intellectual calibre. The lectures established Wiseman's reputation in England.

In 1840 he was made co-adjutor bishop of the Central District and President of Oscott College. And when Pius IX concluded that the time was right to restore the English hierarchy it seemed almost inevitable that Wisemen should be chosen as the first Archbishop of Westminster and given his Cardinal's hat.

Wiseman's purpose in writing about Pius VII was not to write a full biography, nor to offer a chronological history of his reign, but rather to present to English readers human portraits of a Holy Father whom he had known personally and admired, and of the outstanding statesmen, scholars and artists who had formed part of his court.

When the English Catholic hierarchy was restored, *The Times* thundered against Papal aggression. In 1854, at a magnificent ceremony in Rome attended by fifty-one cardinals, and two hundred bishops, the doctrine of the Immaculate Conception of Our Lady was proclaimed as an article of Faith. The people of Rome were jubilant, the city was illuminated, and the bishops were escorted home with torches. As Wiseman indicates in the present work, ultra-montanism was "increasing on every side"

While to some this was a source of great joy, to others, especially many in the English-speaking world, it was something of which they were wary. Wiseman believed that greater personal knowledge of the popes as human beings would bring an increase in affectionate sentiment which would help mature attitudes towards the formal

INTRODUCTION iv

truths of the Faith. It was undoubtedly the sympathy which many Englishmen had felt for Pius VII in his struggles with Napoleon that had helped make the climate propitious for Catholic Emancipation in 1829. Wiseman seems to have wished to recapture some of that spirit. To those who knew him well he was a man of strong personal feelings. His biographer, Wilfrid Ward speaks of "his childlike simplicity" and of his "sensitiveness and affectionateness, in some instances so great as to appear incompatible with the robuster qualities demanded by his position."

It is this side to him which Wiseman reveals in his recollections. But because he was a church statesman, he also provides a fascinating picture of Rome in the days of Pius VII, and the way this Pope and his ministers reformed the government of the Papal States and faced down Napoleon. It is all the more interesting that Wiseman also reveals his admiration for Napoleon as a civil reformer, and as someone who had brought France back from the horrors and chaos of the French revolution, and of the Terror which followed. We need to remember that Wiseman was writing at the time when Napoleon's relation, Napoleon III, was proving himself to be a stout defender of the Church.

Some comments about the historical background before Pius VII's accession may be useful. Rome in the eighteenth century had been one of the most broadly civilised places in human history. In his great work, *Daily Life in Papal Rome in the 18th century*, Maurice Andrieux shows how this was so in great detail. He writes, "Rome had been at other periods greater in art or in the craft of politics; at no other times was she so engaging or so tranquil. For these hundred years she was a smiling city." It is not surprising that she was the ultimate goal and culmination of the Grand Tour.

But by 1800, when Pius VII commenced his pontificate, the French Revolution and the rise of Napoleon had created political turmoil in Europe. 18th century Popes, who were by most criteria good men, nevertheless had seen little purpose in change. They did not even break with the time-honoured custom whereby, on being elected to the pontificate, they enriched their families and friends.

But Pius VII, who had left family and the world when he became a monk, broke with this tradition and did not gather his family and retainers around him and offer them preferment and wealth on assuming office. As a former monk he continued to live simply. He kept up with his scholarly friends in the little leisure time that he had, and was regularly seen by his subjects taking exercise on his walks out through the Porta Pia.

But by his choice of government ministers Pius demonstrated that he accepted the need for change. Cardinal Consalvi, his Secretary of State during two periods— in the early years of his reign, and after his restoration in 1815,— was one of the most outstanding statesmen of the first part of the 19th century. As Secretary of State he was in charge of internal affairs in Rome and in the Papal States, and also of foreign affairs. He proved to be a master of both.

With the support of Pius VII, Consalvi reorganised the chaotic Papal currency, and introduced a number of far-sighted economic reforms. In foreign affairs Pius VII faced a complex situation. The Papal States and the Church had been fatally weakened by the Treaty of Tolentino in 1797, which had been forced on his predecessor, Pius VI. As Bishop of Ischia in Northern Italy before he became Pope, Pius had winessed at first hand the damage caused by the forces of the French Directorate. He had seen his predecessor, Pius VI, taken into captivity and die in exile at Valence.

And then the balance of power shifted: Imperial Austrian troops drove the French out of much of Northern Italy, so as to make it possible for a papal conclave to meet in Venice under Austrian protection and elect Pius VII as Pope. Very shortly afterwards bands of Neapolitans, with the support of a British naval contingent, reconquered Rome.

Although the French soon regained control of Northern Italy, Napoleon by now was beginning to feel the need for Church support for his wider plans for Europe, and in particular for the process of creating an acceptable system of order and authority. Although a deist himself, he had considerable personal affection for the Church, through his respect for his pious mother, Laetitia. Soon after Pius's election Napoleon sent word to him that he wished to restore the Catholic Church in France.

Pius VII and Cardinal Consalvi worked hard to establish a *modus vivendi* with Napoleon. Consalvi's tactics in his negotiations with Napoleon were brilliant. He saw off Napoleon's attempts at double-dealing, and knew when to stand firm, and when to be flexible. The resulting Concordat of the 15th of July 1801 was a triumph for the Papacy. As a result Pius VII felt able to accept an invitation to Paris to be present at the coronation of Napoleon as Emperor, although in the end Napoleon decided to crown himself.

This proved to be the high point of Napoleon's relations with the Church and the Papal States. On Consalvi's advice, Pius refused to accept the Continental System which would have required him to deny the use of Papal ports to the shipping and trade of enemies of France (especially Great Britain). The Pope clearly wanted to maintain the Papal States' tradition of neutrality in European affairs. But another factor may have been Consalvi's sympathy for the British, because as a young man he had been a protégé of the Cardinal Henry Stuart, Duke of York, the younger brother of Bonnie Prince Charlie.

Pius attempted to appease Napoleon by agreeing to accept Consalvi's resignation as Secretary of State. The attempt failed. In 1809 French troops, under the command of General Radet, broke into the Quirinal Palace. They kidnapped the Pope and Cardinal Pacca, whom the Pope had appointed as Pro-Secretary of State after the loss of

Consalvi, and took them both into exile in France, where they were imprisoned.

It was now that Pius showed his overall firmness of purpose. He excommunicated Napoleon before leaving Rome as the French tricolour was being raised over the Castel San Angelo. He and Consalvi, who had remained in Rome having accepted the minor post of Prefect of the Signature, entered into a policy of non-cooperation with Napoleon. In due course Consalvi was also expelled from Rome, and settled in Paris where he led the policy of courteous non-compliance.

In 1810, the situation came to a head. Napoleon's wife Josephine had failed to provide him with a son, so he decided to divorce her, having first secured the agreement of the Emperor of Austria to marry his daughter, Marie-Louise. Since the French Civil Code allowed divorce, the French Senate was persuaded to annul his marriage to Josephine. In the eyes of the Church, however, Napoleon's marriage to her was valid and indissoluable. The Pope knew that Napoleon and Josephine had been married in church by Cardinal Fesch the day before the coronation. A large minority of the cardinals in Paris boycotted this second marriage to Marie Louise, which was again conducted by Cardinal Fesch.

Napoleon was furious at the Pope's refusal to recognise his second marriage, and at those cardinals like Consalvi who had snubbed his elaborate church wedding. The dissenting cardinals were deprived of their property, had their right to wear the Cardinal's red clerical dress in Paris withdrawn, and were exiled from Paris. In retaliation the Pope refused to invest any new bishops in France (in 1811 there were 27 vacant bishoprics). Napoleon had the conditions of the Pope's imprisonment tightened, hoping to break his spirit.

The Emperor then summoned a great council of his French bishops in an attempt to have new bishops appointed without the Pope's consent. It refused to operate without the Pope. Napoleon made further attempts to win the Pope round, but although he momentarily agreed to compromise, as Wiseman indicates in his account, Pius later retracted this offer, and the stalemate continued.

Napoleon's defeats in Moscow and at Leipzig followed, and Wellington's triumphs over the French in Spain. Much weakened, Napoleon again sought a deal with the Pope. He had him moved to comfortable quarters at Fontainbleau, perhaps because he was afraid that Pius might be rescued by the English while he was campaigning elsewhere.

Wiseman gives much of the detail of the process by which the Pope and Cardinal Consalvi, reappointed as Secretary of State, finally effected an almost complete restoration of the Pope's rule in the Papal States. These events had happened only a few years before Wiseman's arrival in Rome, and the true facts were well known. The combination of the Pope's great goodness and his personal suffering resulting from his long struggle with Napoleon had evoked widespread sympathy among the leaders of the other European powers. It was Consalvi's great skill, using the friendships which he had forged with the Prince Regent and Castlereagh, that turned this sympathy into a diplomatic triumph.

Here is a remarkable case study in the art of diplomacy, as well as a rebuttal of the cynics' view about political leaders. Most of us will now conclude that the Holy Father, as the Vicar of Our Lord, and as the successor of St Peter, is better off without the encumbrances, temptations and compromises inevitable in temporal rule. Yet it is still possible to learn something of value from the gracious way in which authority was exercised, public works fostered, and scholarship and the sciences encouraged, in the days of Pius VII's temporal rule of Rome and the Papal States.

ANTONY MATTHEW

CHAPTER I

THE AUTHOR'S FIRST ARRIVAL IN ROME

I T was on the 18th of December, 1818, that the writer of this volume arrived in Rome in company with five other youths, sent to colonise the English College in that city, after it had been desolate and uninhabited during almost the period of a generation.

This was long before a single steamer had appeared in the Mediterranean, or even plied between the French and English coasts. The land-journey across France, over the Alps and down Italy, was then a formidable undertaking, and required appliances, personal and material, scarcely compatible with the purposes of their journey. A voyage by sea from Liverpool to Leghorn was therefore considered the simplest method of conveying a party of ten persons from England to Italy.

It is not the purpose of this work to describe the adventures and perils, at which many might smile, of "the middle passage" and subsequent travel. It will be sufficient to say that the embarkation took place on the 2nd of October, and the arrival late in December; that, of this period, a fortnight was spent in beating up from Savona to Genoa, and another week in running from Genoa to Livorno; that a man fell overboard and was drowned off Cape St. Vincent; that a dog went raving mad on board, from want of fresh water, and luckily, after clearing the decks, jumped or slipped into the sea; that the vessel was, once at least, on fire; and that all the passengers were nearly lost in a sudden squall in Ramsay Bay, into which they had been driven by stress of weather, and where they of course landed.

The reader, who may now make the whole journey in four days, will indulgently understand how pleasing must have been to those early travellers' ears the usual indication, by voice and outstretched whip, embodied in the well-known exclamation of every *vetturino*, "Ecco Roma."

To one "*lasso maris et viarum*,"[1] like Horace, these words brought the first promise of approaching rest; the only assurance, after months of homelessness, that the bourn was reached, the harbour attained, where, at least for years to come, he would calmly devote himself to his duties once more welcomed. A few miles only of weary hills—every one of which, when surmounted, gave a more swelling and majestic outline to the great cupola which alone, in the distance, represented "Roma," and cut, like a huge peak, into the clear winter sky,—and the long journey is ended, and ended by the full realisation of well-cherished hopes.

To some, at least, of the six who had that day entered it, while the remainder followed more leisurely, Rome had been no new thought. Before any idea had been entertained of restoring the English College there, its history, its topography, its antiquities, had formed the bond of a little college society devoted to this queen of cities; while the dream of its longings had been the hope of one day seeing what could then be only known through tourists' reports and fabulous plans. How faint must the hope have been of the fulfilment of schemes which involved a voyage of thrice the length of one to America at present, and with its additional land journey, about as long as a circular sail, in a clipper, to New Zealand!

It has been written above, "*maris et viarum*;" for the land-ways were about as perilous as the broad ocean path. For "there be land sharks," or at least there were then, as dangerous as sea-sharks. At the little wretched hotel in Pontedoro, the *vetturino* warned us, unfoundedly we really believe, to lock our doors; and as we communicated by pantomime more than by words as yet, he drew his hand across his thyroid gland with a most amiable expression of countenance. However, at Florence we were of course assured that the

1. Horace: Carmina: 2.6.7. [Tired of the sea and of journeying.]

roads were most unsafe; and two evidences of this met our
eyes, though they carried with them some antidote of comfort. At that moment the dense woods which skirted the
road near Bolsena were, by order of the government, being
cut down to a considerable distance on either side to destroy
the cover of human wolves, and give the traveller a chance
of preparing his defence should they come so far beyond
their favourite retreat; for the bandit is naturally a prowler.
But, further, from time to time we passed tall posts on the
wayside;—not bearing either the festooned garlands of the
vine, or the strained harp-wires of the electric telegraph,
both symbols of peace and harmony, but supporting ghastly
trophies of justice avenged on the spot where crime had
been committed—the limbs, still fresh, of executed outlaws.

Long-standing desires, then, were about to be satisfied
at last, some degree of recent apprehension to be allayed,
and welcome rest after long travel was promised; when, at
the end of the road which looks straight onwards from the
Milvian Bridge, we could see the open gate of Rome.

That noble entrance was then by no means what it now
is. On the outside, the gate of the Borghese villa did not
stand near; but the visitor had to walk a long way under the
wall of the city which overhung his path, till a narrow gate
led him into a close alley, the first in the grounds.

Within the Flaminian Gate, the obelisk indeed was
there, as were the twin churches beyond, closing, by their
porticoes and domes, the edge of houses between the three
great divergent streets; but that was all. The sculptured terraces of Monte Pincio had as yet no existence; this was still
a green hill, scored by unshaded roads and chance-tracked
paths to its more shapely summit. On the opposite side a
long low barrack-building for cavalry formed a slovenly
boundary to the ample square, in which as yet had not risen
the lofty and massive edifices, hotels though they be, which
now close its further end. Still it was one of the grandest
approaches to any modern city, and one that did not altogether deceive you. The slow pace of a *vettura* along the

Corso gives an opportunity of admiring the magnificent palaces that flank it on both sides, till a turn to the right brings you into the square, of which the column of Antoninus forms the centre; and then a twist to the left places you before a row of pillars which also bear his imperial name; but in addition, a more modern one, unpleasant to travellers' ears—that of Custom House. Even this most distasteful department of civilised government contrives in Rome to get lodged in a classical monument of ancient taste.

From this point, after its disagreeable ceremonial had been completed, all reckoning was lost. A long narrow street, and the Pantheon burst full into view; then a labyrinth of tortuous ways, through which a glimpse of a church or palace-front might occasionally be caught askew; then the small square opened on the eye, which, were it ten times larger, would be oppressed by the majestic, over-whelming mass of the Farnese palace, as completely Michelangelesque in brick as the Moses is in marble; and another turn and a few yards of distance placed us at the door of the "venerable English College." Had a dream, after all, bewildered one's mind, or at least closed the eager journey, and more especially its last hours, during which the tension of anxious expectation had wrought up the mind to a thousand fancies? No description had preceeded actual sight. No traveller, since the beginning of the century, or even from an earlier period, had visited or mentioned it. It had been sealed up as a tomb for a generation; and not one of those who were descending from the unwieldy vehicle at its door had collected, from the few lingering patriarchs, once its inmates, who yet survived at home, any recollections by which a picture of the place might have been prepared in the imagination. Having come so far, somewhat in the spirit of sacrifice, in some expectation of having to "rough it," as pioneers for less venturesome followers, it seemed incredible that we should have fallen upon such pleasant places as the seat of future life and occupation. Wide and lofty vaulted corridors; a noble staircase leading to the vast and airy halls succeeding one another; a spacious garden, glowing with the lemon and orange, and presenting to one's first approach a perspective in fresco by Pozzi,—engraved by him in his celebrated work on perspective; a library, airy, large and cheerful, whose shelves, however, exhibited a specimen of what antiquarians call "*opus tumultuarium*," in the piled up disorganised volumes from folio to duodecimo, that crammed them; a refectory, wainscoted in polished walnut, and above that, St. George and the Dragon by the same artist, ready to drop on to the floor from the groined ceiling; still better, a chapel, unfurnished indeed, but illuminated from floor to roof with the saints of England, and with celestial glories, leading to the altar, that had to become the very hearthstone of new domestic attachments and the centre of many yet untasted joys;—such were the first features of our future abode, as, alone and undirected, we wandered through the solemn building, and made it, after years of silence, re-echo to the sound of English voices, and give back the bounding tread of those who had returned to claim their own. And such, indeed, it might well look to them when, after months of being "cribbed, cabined, and confined" in a small vessel, and jammed in a still more tightly packed *vettura*, they found in the upper corridors, wide and airy as those below, just the right number of rooms for their party, clean and speckless, with every article of furniture, simple and collegiate indeed, yet spic-and-span new, and manifestly prepared for their expected arrival.

One felt at once at home; the house belonged to no one else; it was English ground, a part of the fatherland, a restored inheritance. And though all was neat and trim, dazzling in its whiteness relieved here and there by tinted architectural members, one could not but feel that we had been transported to the scene of better men and greater things than were likely to arise in the new era that day opened. Just within the great entrance-door, a small one to the right led into the old church of the Holy Trinity, which wanted but its roof to restore it to use. There it stood, nave and aisles, separated by pillars connected by arches, all in their places, with the lofty walls above them. The altars had been, indeed, removed; but we could trace their forms; and the painted walls marked the frame of the altar-pieces, especially of the noble painting by Durante Alberti, still preserved in the house representing the Patron-Mystery, and St. Thomas of Canterbury, and St. Edward the Martyr. This vision of the past lasted but a few years; for the walls were pronounced unsafe, the old church was demolished, and the unsightly shell of a thoroughly modern church was substituted for the old basilica under the direction of Valadier, a good architect, but one who knew nothing of the feelings which should have guided his mind and pencil in such a work.

It was something however to see, that first day, the spot revisited by English youth where many an English pilgrim, gentle or simple, had knelt, leaning on his trusty staff cut in Needwood or the New Forest; where many a noble student from Bologna or Padua had prayed, as he had been lodged and fed, "*in formâ pauperis,*" when, before returning home, he came to visit the tomb of the Apostles; and, still more, where many and many a student, like those now gathered there, had sobbed farewell to the happy spring days and the quiet home of youth, before starting on his weary journey to the perils of evil days in his native land. Around lay scattered memorials of the past. One splendid monument, erected to Sir Thomas Dereham at the bottom of the church, was entirely walled up and roofed over, and so invisible. Shattered and defaced lay the richly effigied tombs of an Archbishop of York, and a Prior of Worcester, and of many other English worthies: while sadder wreckage of the recent storm was piled on one side—the skulls and bones of, perhaps, Cardinal Allen, F. Persons, and others, whose coffins had been dragged up from the vaults below, and converted into munitions of war.

And if there needed a living link between the present

and the past, between the young generation at the door, and the old one that had passed into the crypt of the venerable church, there it was, in the person of the more than octogenerian porter Vincenzo, who stood, all salutation, from the wagging appendage to his grey head to the large silver buckles on his shoes, mumbling toothless welcomes in a yet almost unknown tongue, but full of humble joy and almost patriarchal affection, on seeing the haunts of his own youth repeopled.

CHAPTER II

THE FIRST AUDIENCE

THIS second chapter, it may be imagined, ought to open with an apology for the first. For, what interest can the reader be supposed to take in its personal details, or what bearing can it have on the subject of this work? The first portion of this question it might be presumptuous to answer; the second is entitled to a reply. A writer who is not going to compile from others, but to give his own impressions, recollections or opinions, who is not composing a history from other people's materials, but seeking to contribute his own share, however slight, to the stock of future collectors, is bound to establish some claim to credit from his readers. If he cannot advance any on the grounds of past diligence or present skill, of careful observation or graphic power, he must at least endeavour to gain that right, which casual circumstances and fortuitous position may confer upon him, to belief and attention.

Now, for any one born within the precincts of the present century to venture on giving his personal observations or recollections of nearly forty years ago, in a distant country, to assert that he had opportunities, from so remote a period down to the present time, not merely of hearing, but of seeing, what can illustrate the character of successive

sovereigns on one throne,—still more, to begin his notes by
stating that, within a few days of his arrival at its seat, he
was familiarly in the presence of its occupant,—gives reason enough for a cautious reader to ask, How came this to
pass, and what can justify belief in such an improbability?

It is the answer to this inquiry that has been attempted
in the first chapter. Not in the garb of a courtier, bred in the
palace-halls, not by privilege of dignity or station, but in
the simple habit of a collegian, and through the claim of fil-
ial rights upon a common father, was secured an early
approach to the feet of the good and holy Pius VII. It certainly makes one feel old when one's life is counted by five
pontificates; but this, to a catholic mind, is surely compensated by the reflection, that each venerated possessor of
that exalted dignity has shed his blessing upon one portion
or other of its existence, from the buoyant and hopeful time
of early youth, to heavier and sadder hours. This unbroken
continuance of a kindness, which amounts to a grace,
required a peculiarity of position that has no claims to
merit, and therefore may be freely mentioned. The pages
which follow will require this freedom, already commenced
in the foregoing chapter; let this one apology suffice for the
volume. Nor will it appear unnatural, that a relation so
established, between condescending goodness on one side
and reverent affection on the other,—a relation which the
reader may call chance, and the writer Providence,—should
be found by the favoured party to have exercised an influence on his pursuits, his thoughts, and the whole direction
of his life.

The event to which the first chapter related—the reestablishment of the suppressed English College in
Rome—was the work, almost spontaneous, of Pius, and
his great minister, Cardinal Consalvi. It may not be unin-
teresting to return to this subject hereafter. For the
present thus much may suffice. Although a rector, and one
fully qualified for his office, had been in possession of the
house for year, the arrival of the colony of students was

the real opening of the establishment. On the day alluded to, the excellent superior, the Rev. Robert Gradwell, on returning home, found the first instalment of this important body really domiciled in his house, to the extent of having converted to present use the preparations for his own frugal meal.

The event was of significant magnitude to be communicated to the secretary of state; and the answer was, that as many of the party as could be provided with the old and hallowed costume of the English College should be presented to the Holy Father within a few days. Among the more fortunate ones was, owing to favourable accident, the present writer.

The feelings of anyone permitted to approach that most venerable man had necessarily a colour and vividness beyond those inspired by his dignity and office. His history had been mixed up with that of the world, and its very anecdotes were fresh in the memory. To the young especially, who remembered him only in a position so different from his natural one—as a captive and a persecuted Pontiff; who had almost learnt to disjoin the idea of the supreme rule of the Church from all the pomp and even power of worldy state, and to associate it with prisons and bonds, as in the early ages—there was around the tiara of Pius the halo of the confessor, that eclipsed all gold and jewels. His portrait had been familiar to us, but it was that, not of a High Priest clad in "the vesture of holiness," but of an aged man bending over the crucifix in search of its consolations, and speaking those words which had been made sacred by his constant utterance—"May the holy and adorable will of God be ever done!"

Then came the news of his wonderful triumphs, his humble victory scarcely less astonishing than that of arms. He had been rescued from his durance, not by the power of man, not by the armies that had almost hemmed in his prison, but by that higher Will, that keeps in its own hands the hearts of kings, and turns them at its pleasure. The

same stern command which had torn him from his palace
and borne him away, had set him free, or rather ordered his
restoration. To this, indeed, had succeeded another danger
and a temporary retreat; so that the final settlement of the
Holy Pontiff in his dominions, and their restoration in their
integrity,[1] had occurred only three years before, and bore
the character of recent events. As yet indeed one might
have said, that the triumphal arches and garlands of his joyful entry into Rome had scarcely faded, and that the echoes
of the cries of welcome that greeted him, still lingered
among the seven hills. For the people all spoke of them as
things of yesterday.

It was not therefore "being presented to the Pope," as the
current phrase runs, that awaited us, at least in the ordinary
sense. To every catholic, and to a young ecclesiastic in particular, this must be an event in his life: and the ceremony
combined a double feeling, elsewhere impossible, composed
of reverence paid to a sovereign and the homage due to the
supreme head of our religion. From the monarch we accept
a condescending word; from the Pope that word we receive
as a blessing. When to the natural emotions thus inspired
by the union in one person of the double rank of sovereignty and supremacy, we add the more individual sentiment
which the personal character of Pope Pius VII excited in
our minds, it will be easily conceived, that our hearts beat
with more than usual speed, and not without some flurry, as
we ascended the great staircase of the Quirinal Palace on
Christmas-eve, the day appointed for the audience. This is
a different entrance from the one now generally used. After
passing through the magnificent *Sala Regia*, you proceed
through a series of galleries adorned with fine old tapestry,
and other works of art, though furnished with the greatest
simplicity. The last of these was the antechamber to the
room occupied by the Pope. After a short delay, we were
summoned to enter this; a room so small that it scarcely

1. By the Treaty of Vienna, 9th of June, 1815.

allowed space for the usual genuflections at the door, and in the middle of the apartment. But instead of receiving us, as was customary—seated—the mild and amiable Pontiff had risen to welcome us, and meet us, as we approached. He did not allow it to be a mere presentation, or a visit of ceremony. It was a fatherly reception, and in the truest sense our inauguration into the duties that awaited us. It will be best, however, to give the particulars of this first interview with the occupant of St. Peter's Chair in the words of a memorandum entered, probably that day, in the Rector's journal.

"Dec. 25. Took six of the students to the Pope. The other four could not be clothed. The Holy Father received them standing, shook hands with each, and welcomed them to Rome. He praised the English clergy for their good and peaceful conduct, and their fidelity to the Holy See. He exhorted the youths to learning and piety, and said; 'I hope you will do honour both to Rome and to your own country.' "

Such is the writer's first recollection of a Pope, and that Pope the illustrious Pius VII. Whatever we had read of the gentleness, condescension, and sweetness of his speech, his manner, and his expression, was fully justified, realised, and made personal. It was not from what we had heard, but from what we had seen and experienced, that we must needs now revere and love him. The friendly and almost national grasp of the hand—(after due homage had been willingly paid)—between the Head of the Catholic Church, venerable by his very age, and a youth who had nothing even to promise; the first exhortation on entering a course of ecclesiastical study—its very inaugural discourse, from him who was believed to be the fountain of spiritual wisdom on earth;—these surely formed a double tie, not to be broken, but rather strength-ened by every subsequent experience.

I know not how a dignitary of any other religion, though holding no royal power and majesty, would receive a body of youths about to devote themselves to the service of his creed; nor whether he would think it worth while to admit them at all to an interview. But to Rome there flock, from every region of the earth, aspirants to the ecclesiastical state, in boyhood, and well-nigh in childhood, speaking as many languages as were used by the Apostles on the day of Pentecost; and yet perhaps hardly one of them fails to come into personal contact with him, to whom from infancy he has looked up, as the most exalted personage in the world. Soon after his first arrival he receives an early blessing on his future career, accompanied often with a few kind words, unfailingly with a benign look. That brief moment is an epoch in life, perhaps a starting point for success. In addition to the general attachment that united him with millions to the Head of his Church, there is established a personal bond, an individual connection. It is no longer awe and distant reverence, but an affection as distinct in character as that to one intimately related. And this relation is strengthened in the youthful mind at every succeeeding year of his course. He knows that every professor whose lectures he hears has been directly and immediately appointed, after careful selection, by the Pope himself, and that every class-book which he reads has received the same supreme sanction; he feels himself almost under the direct tuition of the Holy See, however pure and sparkling the rills at which others may drink, he puts his lips to the very rock which a divine wand has struck, and he sucks in its waters as they gush forth living.

But does he, in his turn, preach in the papal chapel, in accordance with the privilege, which may be exercised by each college, on some important feast?—he is separately presented to the Holy Father, and receives a paternal and gracious compliment. Does he give a public demonstration of his ability or application, by holding, as it is called, a thesis, that is, against all comers to test his prowess, at the close of his philosophical or theological studies?—still more is he entitled, as the very guerdon of his success, to lay at the feet of him whose doctrines he has openly maintained and defended the printed articles on which he has stood trial, and to hear kind encouraging words, which compensate for his

months of toilsome preparation, and his day of anxious struggle. Finally, when his career is finished, and he is about to
pass from the period of probation and peaceful preparation to
the labour of the field, its burthen and its heat, he never fails
to obtain a parting audience, at which he solicits, and
obtains, a benediction on his future work. And seldom does
it happen that he leaves the Eternal City without having
obtained, at one or other of those more special interviews,
some token, direct from the hand which he kisses,—a medal,
or rosary, or cross, which is treasured through life, and renews
almost daily into freshness the associations of youth.

Nor does it seldom happen that one finds one's self
remembered from a previous interview, and a question is
asked which shows the kind tenacity of memory through
which things of higher interest must have passed in the
interval. Is it wonderful that what is unmeaningly called
"ultramontanism" should increase on every side? For what
in reality is it? Not, certainly, a variation of doctrine, but a
more vivid and individual perception,— an experience, of
its operation. The "supremacy" is believed by the untrav-
elled as by the travelled catholic. Facilities of access, and
many other causes, have increased the number of those
who have come into contact with successive Pontiffs: and
this contact has seldom failed to ripen an abstract belief
into an affectionate sentiment: but with those who have
continued for years under the same influence, unvarying in
its winning and impressive forms, it becomes a fixed element constant and persevering where all else may differ,
and gives warmth and strength to their religious and ecclesiastical convictions. The German student will carry away
his Roman impressions, theorised perhaps in a more
abstruse and transcendental form, the Frenchman will bear
them in a more imaginative and poetical shape; to the
English mind they will present themselves more practical-
ly, and as guides to action; while perhaps the American
will relish them the more keenly because they contrast so
strongly with whatever he most admires in secular and

temporal policy, and bear the seal of a distinct order of existence. But all, whithersoever they go, will belong to the school in which they have been educated, and naturally communicate their own feelings to many.

This chapter, as much as the first, may seem to require an apology for irrelevancies. If so, let this be the apology. It shows how much more close, than may at first appear, is the bond which may unite an insignificant person with the most exalted one in the world of faith—how many may be the opportunites of observation, and how vivid the impressions, which may give one a right to portray the other.

CHAPTER III

CHARACTER OF PIUS THE SEVENTH

I T would be difficult to imagine a countenance that more faithfully brings to the surface the inward character, or a character that more fully and undisguisedly displays itself in the features, than those of this venerable Pontiff. And it is not too much to say, that rarely has a more successful portrait come from the pencil of an artist than that of him by Sir Thomas Lawrence. This eminent painter arrived in Rome in May, 1819, with a commission to take the likenesses of the Pope and of Cardinal Consalvi;[1] —the one as represented, the other as his representative, at the Congress of Vienna. It was not, therefore, altogether a personal compliment; for the two portraits form portions of a series containing all the sovereigns, and their ambassadors, who took part in that momentous assembly. Most readers will have admired it yet existing in Windsor Castle. [2]

But the writer had the advantage of seeing these two admirable pictures when exhibited, by the artist himself, under the roof which covered their originals—the

1. His portrait is now in the Waterloo Chamber, Windsor Castle.
2. Now in the Queen's Gallery, London

Quirinal Palace, and of thus judging of their accuracy. Among the multitudes that flocked to view them, there was but one opinion, that they were perfect likenesses, not merely such as copy the features, but such as transmit to posterity the expression, character, a feeling of the person represented. Of the Pope, of course, many portraits had been taken during the previous nineteen years of his chequered pontificate, but none that approached to this, or gave him living to the world. Of the Cardinal this was the first representation from life. A friend of the author's called on the Cardinal to present his credentials at the very moment that Sir Thomas was with him, on the 13th of May, and the Cardinal introduced them to one another. His Eminence said that he had always been averse to having his portrait taken, but added, showing him Lord Castlereagh's letter, "However, what can I do in this case? It is impossible to refuse."

Although the eyes of Italian critics were open to the characteristic defects of Sir Thomas's manner, and naturally blamed his apparent negligence in secondary parts, and his neglect even of accuracy in accessories, the heads were acknowledged to be faultless, and brilliantly successful. The pose of the body, sunk unelastic into the chair, and seeking support from its arms, the wearied stoop and absence of energy in the limbs and head, tell us of seventy-seven years, among which had been some of calamity and grief. And yet the hair, scarcely bearing a trace of time, or of that more violent hand which has often been known to do in one night the work of years, but black and flowing, the forehead still smooth and unfurrowed by wrinkles, the mouth not dragged-down, but clearly impressed with an habitual smile, show the serene and enduring mind with which the vicissitudes of a long life had been passed—a life of rare passages and changes,—from a noble home to a cloister; from the cowl to the mitre; from the bishopric to the See of Peter; then from Savona palace to the dungeon; and now, at last, again from Savona to Rome. That there should be lassitude, and even feebleness, marked in that frame and on that countenance, can excite no wonder; but that there should be not one symptom of soured temper, or bitter recollection, or unkind thought, nay, not even of remembered humiliation and anguish, is proof not only of a sweet disposition, but of a well-tutored and well governed mind, and of strong principles capable of such guiding power.

The life of a sovereign generally dates from his accession to the throne. It is by reigns that the world's history is written. The man is nothing to mankind, the king everything to the nation. What he was before the commencement of his royal career is scarcely recorded or faintly remembered; for it is not taught to the children. To have a place for anterior honours in a country's annals he must die before reaching that throne which will eclipse them all. A Black Prince, or a Princess Charlotte, had the best friend to their early fame in death. A royal crown will cover over and hide an immense quantity of laurels.

Scire piget, post tale decus, quid fecerit ante. [1]

is as true of a coronation as of Scaevola's exploit.[2]

Hence, in general, there is very little curiosity about the antecedents of the successor to the pontifical throne, although they may be very important for estimating subsequent character. This is certainly the case with Pius VII. That he was a man so meek and gentle, so incapable of rancour or resentment, that Cardinal Pacca's scruples not to apply to him the inspired words descriptive of Moses, "that he was the mildest of men," no one has ever questioned. This particular quality may be called the very grace of his nature, so distinctly was it stamped on his outward appearance, so penetratingly diffused through the actions of his life.

No one, moreover, will refuse to him that strength which

1. [It is unpleasant to get to know what he did before, after such glory.]
2. Quintus Mucius Scaevola, the legendary Roman figure who, when captured, thrust his right hand in the fire, to show his indifference to death.

is the companion often of the gentlest disposition, a power of unrepining endurance, the patent fortitude which suffers without complaint and without sullenness.

But qualities of a much higher order belong to him, and yet have been overlooked. Nor has the course of his earlier life been sufficiently brought forward, to explain or illustrate the peculiar character which he afterwards displayed.

The basis of this must be considered as deeply laid in the very first inspirations of childhood. If nature gave to Barnabas Chiaramonti a mild and sweet disposition, a higher influence bestowed upon him a better gift. Religion invested him with the beauty of an unsullied life, with a character of irreproachable virtue throughout his length of days. Few familes in Europe are more illustrious than his; but, while from his father he derived high nobility, from his mother, daughter of Marchese Ghini, he received a more valuable portion, that of rare piety and virtue. She was, indeed, a lady of singular excellence,[1] renowned in the world for every religious quality. After having com-

---

1. The archdeacon Hyacinth Ignatius Chiaramonti, brother of Pius, published in 1786, and dedicated to him, then cardinal, a Latin poem, "*De majorum suorum laudibus*," ("In Praise of our Elders") in which he thus addresses their mother:—

> "*O semper memoranda parens! O carmine nostro*
> *Non unquam laudata satis! me despice clemens,*
> *Exutumque tibi mortali corpore junge:*
> *Sit, precor, haec merces, nostrorum haec meta laborum.*"

["We must remember you for ever who brought us into the world. You can never be sufficiently praised in our verses. Look down on me with kindness, and when I am stripped bare unite me to you in my mortal body, and let this be, I pray, the reward and goal of our labours."]

I remember it used to be said at Rome, and I have read the same assurance since, that only the resolute opposition of the son, when elevated to the supreme pontificate, prevented the more solemn recognition, by beatification, of the extraordinary sanctity of the mother.

pleted the education of her children, when the future
Pontiff had reached the age of twenty-one, in 1763, she
entered a convent of Carmelites at Fano, where her memory is still cherished, and where she died in 1771, at the
age of sixty. It was in this retreat that, as Pius himself used
to relate, she distinctly foretold him his elevation one day
to the papacy, and the protracted course of sufferings
which it would entail.

These earliest impressions of domestic examples and mater-
nal teaching formed, as has been said, the very ground-work
of Pius' character. At the age of sixteen, after a preliminary
education in the college for nobles at Ravenna, he retired,
upon mature deliberation, to the Benedictine Abbey of Santa
Maria del Monte, near Cesena, his native city. There could be
no worldly motive for this step. He had nothing to fly from in
his home. His birth and patrimony secured him earthly comfort. If he inclined merely to the ecclesiastical life, all its
advantages were open to him as a secular priest, without sepa-
ration from his family, in which he was well-beloved. And
certainly, if honourable promotion in the world had been,
even slightly, an object of his ambition, he was cutting off
every chance of it which his connections, or his efforts, might
have secured him in the secular state.

A twofold discipline, preparatory to his future life, such as
Providence had designed it, awaited him in the cloister. The
first was the discipline of the monastic noviciate, the sinking
of all rank and titles; the renouncing of all fortune, luxury
and money; the voluntary descent to a level of rude equality
with the peasant's or artisan's son; the surrender of comforts
in every change,—passing from the paintings and tapestries
of the ancestral palace to the bare corridors of the monastery;
from the chatty society of the table to the silent feeding of
the body in the refectory; from the neat chamber, with its
elastic bed and damask curtains, to the whitewashed cell,
with its straw pallet and plank shutters; the menial occupations of a household—being one's own servant, and doing
everything for oneself; and finally the utter subjection with

ready cheerfulness of time, actions, will, to the guidance of the
rule and of obedience. For any one who sees the youthful aspirants to the religious institutes here or abroad, in recreation or at
study, may easily decide who will persevere, by a very simple
rule. The joyous faces, and the sparkling eyes, denote the future
monks far more surely than the demure looks and stolen glances.

In the days of Pius' distress, all his previous discipline came
admirably to his aid. He had commenced it at sixteen; had
dropped his high-sounding names of Barnabas Chiaramonti
for simple Don Gregory (first, indeed, only Brother); made
but one of a party, clothed alike, and without distinction,
beyond that of the assumed monastic name. He walked the
streets, and was jostled in crowds, and probably could not
have paid for a cool refreshment. It was in this way that he
hastened to the square of St. Peter's to witness the coronation
of Clement XIV. This imposing ceremony is performed in the
loggia, whence the Pope gives his benediction, looking into
the superb esplanade densely thronged. Eager to get a sight of
the spectacle, and clear himself of the throng, he leapt up
behind an empty carriage. The coachman turned round, but
instead of resenting this intrusion on his dominions, said
good-naturedly to him, "My dear little monk, why are you so
anxious to see a function which one day will fall to your lot?"[1]

The sincerity of this vocation was fully tried. Pope Pius VI,
his immediate predecessor, was a great friend of the family.
Wishing to promote to high dignity some one belonging to
it, he selected another brother, Gregory, whom he called to
Rome, and placed in the "Ecclesiastical Academy," an establishment for the education of youths preparing for public life.
This preference, due to the choice being made by Barnabas
of the monastic state, cut off all hopes of his preferment, had
they ever existed in his mind. The title of abbot was all that
the Pope himself could procure for him, with some difficulty,
in the way of honour and distinction.

1. The authority for this anecdote is the Pope's learned secretary, Monsignor Testa, who told the author he had heard it from the Pope.

It will be easy to trace the influence of this severe and early schooling upon the conduct of Pius in his day of hardship and sorrow. He was as a man already acquainted with these things. A condition which might have embarassed him, or worn him down, or added to the weight of public griefs those petty annoyances which still more oppressively tease and fret, presented to him only analogies with the life to which he had accustomed himself, and was treated with comparative lightness of heart.

When he was suddenly and rudely forced from his palace in the night of June 6, 1809, thrust into a carriage, and whirled away through the dust and heat of an Italian summer-day, without an attendant, "without linen—without his spectacles;" fevered and wearied, he never for a moment lost his serenity. *"Nos deux voyageurs"* (Pius VII and Cardinal Pacca) *"répondent à mes procédés pour eux, et rient quelquefois avec nous;"* writes General Radet, in a letter brutal and vulgar in its tone addressed to General Miollis, the morning after the first day's distressing travel.[1] Nay, Cardinal Pacca amusingly tells us that, when they had just started on this most dismal of journeys, the Pope asked him if he had any money. The secretary of state replied, that he had had no opportunity of providing himself. "We then drew forth our purses," continued the cardinal, "and notwithstanding the state of affliction we were in at being thus torn away from Rome, and all that was dear to us, we could hardly compose our countenances, on finding the contents of each purse to consist—of the Pope's, of a *papetto* (10p.), and of mine, of three *grossi* (7.5p.). We had precisely thirty-five *bajocchi* between us. The Pope, extending his hand, showed his *papetto* to General Radet, saying, at the same time,'Look here—this is all I possess.' "[1] Truly, *"Ils rient quelquefois avec*

---

1. Published in Chevalier Artaud's *Life of Pius VIII*, p.295. It had come to light only about 1844. This letter is alluded to in the same General's apologetic epistle to Pius VII, dated September 12th, 1814, published at the end of Cardinal Pacca's *Memoirs*.

nous." A good joke i' faith; a monarch smiling at finding himself penniless; and the man to whom he smiles sees no beauty or sublimity in the smile, nor in the simple words which explain it—no! it is only a proper item for an official report, as showing how completely he has done his work.[1]

So much for money and any care about it. The august traveller was without even a change of clothes or of linen. And later still, when no longer in the hands of men like Radet, he was in possession of only one dress, a stuff cassock, given to him by the King of Spain, totally unsuited to the season in which he was obliged to wear it. This he mentioned to a friend, an Englishman at Rome, in 1820, from whom I derive this statement. Indeed those who have desired to lower him before the world, have dwelt particularly on the want of dignity which they discovered in his performing for himself common menial services, and even mending his own garments. They have set him down, for this, as a craven and poor-spirited creature, endowed with no sense of honour, pride and self-respect.

There can be no doubt that in all this there is nothing dramatic nor, in the vulgar sense, heroic. Such a prisoner, such a captive, creates no scenes, gives no impassioned pictures for the pencil or the pen. You cannot invest him with the pathos of St. James or the Temple, nor get soft or tender speeches, or dialogues, out of him; nor—with the dignity of two hundred and fifty-three Pontiff predecessors

1. Cardinal Pacca's *Memoirs*, in Sir G. Head's translation. Cardinal Wiseman notes many inaccuracies in the translation, both of Italian and Latin. He singles out in Vol. ii. p. 302: "Illustrious is that name in the festivals of the Church." No doubt, Wiseman remarks, (he did not have the original at hand) the word in Italian is *fasti* (annals) not *feste* (festivals). On p. 333 he notes that: "*of Dr. Massimo S. Girolamo*" should be "of the greatest of doctors St. Jerome." And on p. 157 he mentions that Tertullian's words: "*Novi pastores in pace leones, in proelio cervos*" had been mistranslated. Head translates "*Novi pastores*" as "new pastors," instead of "*I have known pastors.*" Wiseman notes that "knew" and "new" are both represented in Latin by "*novi,*" but that it is important to make sense of the words by the context!

on his head, with the privileges of the first fisherman, whose ring he wore, inseparable from his very title; and with the firm conviction, or rather consciousness, that he held the very thunder of spiritual might undivided in his hands, from Him whose vicar his captors owned him to be—can one outburst of noble scorn, as the world will call it, one blighting defiance, one solemn appeal to the faith, however drugged to sleep, of those around him, be detailed, or really be discovered, among the records of his captivity. Romance or poetry could not presume to seize on it, as they have done on that of Duguesclin,[1] or Surrey,[2] or King Richard.[3] For there is nothing that the imagination can feed on, or enlarge, or elevate. It is the entire simplicity, naturalness, and unaffected submission to the will of God, without an effort to excite sympathy, diminish severity, or strike out an effect, that constitute the singular beauty of this touching episode.

In the history of the first Charles it is recorded that, when brought to Windsor, on his way to trial and execution, he was for the first time deprived of the kingly state with which he had been served, even during his previous captivity. "This absence of ceremony," says Lingard, "made on the unfortunate monarch a deeper impression than could have been expected. It was, he said, the denial of that to him, which by ancient custom was due to many of his

1. Bertrand Duguesclin was a renowned 14th century French writer and statesman who was responsible for the eviction of the English from Normandy. When he died beseiging Randam in 1388, the Governor of the town insisted on putting the keys of the town on his coffin.
2. Henry Howard, Earl of Surrey, was one of the foremost poets of the 16th century; he was beheaded after falling out with King Henry VIII over his actions in a military campaign in France.
3. King Richard I, after his crusading exploits in the Holy Land, was ship-wrecked in Italy; after wandering in the guise of a pilgrim he was captured by the Duke of Austria and held a prisoner there until he was ransomed by his subjects.

subjects; and rather than submit to the humiliation, he chose to diminish the number of dishes, and to take his meals in private."[1]

I remember reading, many years ago, the narrative written by the Infanta of Spain,[2] of her expulsion or flight from Madrid; and being struck by the pathetic terms in which she records the day whereon, for the first time in her life, she took her meal off earthenware, feeling it an immense hardship, for one who had never, since her birth, eaten from anything less costly than gold plate.

In strong contrast with such examples of pitiful murmuring stands the uncomplaining and cheerful traveller from Rome to Savona. For, indeed, he had been trained for privation and suffering. "Behold, they who are clothed in soft raiment are in the houses of kings."[3] Such was the royal Stuart, such was the gentle Bourbon. But Pius had been educated in the rough habit and with the plain diet of the monk, in fastings often, and in watchings, and in many trials of subjection and obedience. It is not difficult to live over again our earlier life: the officer easily plays the soldier in battle, a painter never forgets how to sketch. And so the monk, in his simplicity and habits of endurance, had lived in Pius though episcopacy, cardinalate, and papacy. During the first two he had not even changed the colour of his robes, symbolical of a mourning and penitential life. Nor had the tiara obliterated the religious crown, shaven on the day of his clothing as a child of St. Benedict, in symbol of that thorny crown which sovereign and monk are equally called to wear. Old as he now was, the days easily came back, when he was girded by another, and led whither this one willed; when his wardrobe was scanty and scarcely his own, and when he had no servant at his beck; but he knew well how to serve himself and, if needful, others. "*Redire in*

1. Dr. Lingard's *History of England*: Charles I, Chapter III, 5th Edition.
2. Afterwards Queen of Etruria.,
3. A paraphrase of the Vulgate text of St. Luke: 7.5.25.

naturam puerorom," to become as little children, is more difficult for a grown man, than it was for a sovereign like Pius to return to his noviciate, whether he was cooped up in a tight well-closed carriage on the road to Radicofani, or in a prison on the Mediterranean. It is surely proof of great stolidity in the general to write, speaking of this journey: "*Je les tiens comme en cage*," forgetting that a carriage, though locked up, does not make, any more than "iron bars, a cage;" and not to put another reading on the occasional smile of his prisoners than he did, and write instead; "*ils se rient parfois de nous.*"

In fact, this previous life of absolute abandonment to the care of Providence; of total ignorance whence the very necessities of life were provided, but of certainty that something would be found; of day-by-day attention to spiritual or intellectual things, without domestic solicitudes or secular cares, that had filled up the monastic period of the Pope's life; was only the practical illustration of a principle which his early piety taught him at his mother's knee—of reliance on God, and simple surrender to His will. Thus ripened and strengthened, the principle must have become one of boundless trustfulness and unwavering faith. It was a confidence, without anxiety, in Him who feeds the fowls of the air and clothes the grass of the field. But under what circumstances? It was indeed a trust in Him who bountifully caters for the sparrow, but felt and expressed when the poor bird was in the claws of the kite. It was hope in Him who arrays His lilies more splendidly than Solomon in all his glory; but sure and full, when the scythe was already levelled by the mower, bending to the stroke.

Hence the captivity of Pius VII is no drama, nor is he a hero. For each is more. The one is a holy history in the annals of the Church, ay, and in those of human virtue. It is changing the light of a picture, taking it out of the glaring and garish brightness of mid-day into a darker and cooler evening atmosphere. All around is subdued and still, and the colouring becomes mellower, and small details almost disappear, and even the expression looks more placid and more grave. But every feature is there, and the character is unchanged: the same the smile, the same the tender eye, and the speaking lip. No grand peculiarities are developed: the beauty is the absence of change. And he who is said to be no hero is much more. There is something almost awful in the unruffled calm which pervades the narrative of nearly continuous imprisonments in the latter portion of Acts. St. Paul is confined at Philippi and Jerusalem, Caesarea and Rome, warily guarded, as an important person, now by sea and by land. But it is all given as a matter of course. No particulars of the gaol, no description of the dungeon, scarcely an incident of years spent by him, girt with a chain, or in free custody. Above all, no account of how he bore it, none of his looks, his words, his sufferings; none of his patience, his cheerfulness, his prayer, his union with Christ. We are supposed to understand all this, and not to require telling that St. Paul in the stocks of the inner dungeon of Philippi, singing God's praises, was the same as St. Paul speaking with noble courage before Festus; that it was a privilege of the apostolic character to be as serene in a dungeon as gracious on the episcopal chair. And so, in course of time, when the lesser details and spare anecdotes of Pius's captivity shall have been first diluted, then melted away in the growing mass of historic material, the writer of his abridged life will find it sufficient to say that he bore his captivity, its perhaps intentional rigour, its accidental aggravations, and its occupational insults, as became his high dignity and noblest inheritance, and in the character and spirit of an apostle.

As the monastic training prepared the Pontiff for one most important portion of his pontifical duties particularly destined for him by Divine Providence, so it did not fail in another, and no less momentous, point.

It has been a generally received opinion, at least one has heard it again and again expressed, that the qualities of the heart prevailed in Pius VII to the almost exclusion of intellectual gifts. Kindness and benevolence, forgiveness and meekness, have been the characteristics by which he has been generally known, and for which he has been universally esteemed. But, however remarkable this gentleness of nature, it was by no means an usurper of his entire character. Though not possessed of genius, nor perhaps of over-average abilities, what he had were fully cultivated and vigorously employed. It is far from being the object of this work to reproduce matter already published, or load its pages by long quotations. It will be, therefore, sufficient to refer to Cardinal Pacca's excellent memoirs for a fuller explanation on this subject. He traces, indeed, to this mistaken apprehension of the Pope's character, the afflicting collision which ensued between the two greatest spheres of spiritual and of temporal power—the see of Rome and the empire of France. But one sentence says so much to our present purpose, and will spare so much less authoritative treatment of the subject, that it will be well to quote it. After remarking that, having been associated with the Pontiff under such varieties of situation, it would have been impossible for his character to have remained disguised from him, the cardinal thus proceeds:—"Having, therefore, attentively studied his character, and well knowing his disposition, I can affirm that Pius VII was by no means deficient in talent, nor of weak, pusillanimous nature. On the contrary, he was a man of ready wit, lively, more than commonly versed in the sacred sciences, and especially possessed of that peculiar description of good sound sense that in matters of business intuitively perceives the difficulties to be overcome, and sees everything in its proper light."[1]

With these words before me, it would scarcely have been too much to attribute to Pope Pius a higher class of abilities than has been just assigned to him. But it is more to the purpose to state how they were cultivated. D. Gregory

1.Vol. ii. p. 43.

Chiaramonti began young, and therefore was able to pass with deliberate leisure through the long and full monastic course of philosophical and theological studies.That he did this with at least a fair success, is evident from the fact of his having publicly sustained a thesis in theology—an experiment not usually accorded to persons of inferior skill. The propositions or programme of his public contest were engraved, as the custom used to be, at the foot of a large allegorical print; and the thesis was dedicated to Cardinal Ganganelli.[1] Thus two future popes met together, the one as patron and the other as client, on the noble field of science. A copy of this challenge was, I know, in the English College library; it was curious, and made itself remembered by the circumstance that one of the subjects proposed in it was the confutation of an absurd fanatic, who had maintained that no place is found in heaven for the daughters of Eve. And this was only one of many occasions in which he made public display of his learning and ready prowess.

After this he was a learned public professor in the colleges of his order, first at Parma, then at Rome. At the age of thirty he was promoted, in general chapter, lector or doctor of theology; and for six years more held the chair of canon law. It would have been impossible, in such a body as the Benedictines of that period in Italy, for any one to have been thus advanced, and intrusted with the highest teaching, unless he had proved himself fully competent. Not only must he have given evidence of his proficiency in the sciences which he was appointed to teach, but he must by this exercise, continued for so many years, have acquired greater maturity of judgment, stronger power of reasoning, and acuter penetration into character, and shrewder knowledge of men. For the scholastic system, as it is called, of instruction brings out the character of the individual pupil, as it keeps constantly well whetted, by discussion, the genius of the professor. Hence, a person

1. later Clement XIV.

who lived for years in constant intercourse with many who
often saw the Pope, and knew him familiarly, used to say,
that while he was reverenced and loved by all that
approached him, he was no less respected for his assiduity
and ability in public affairs. Indeed, during the latter years of
his pontificate, to which these recollections belong, many
questions relating to Great Britain and her colonies had to
be discussed. Step by step the Holy Father himself was
referred to, and took a personal interest in them, and
indeed, entered fully into them; so that the respectable English ecclesiastic alluded to, who frequently himself saw the
Pope on such subjects, has left many records behind him of
the judicious and definite views which he took of them, necessarily new, and even strange as they were, to Rome.

CHAPTER IV

CONTINUATION

THE simplicity of habits, which proved so valuable in
sustaining the amiable Pontiff through the more pitiful vicissitudes of his reign, never left him after he
had ascended the throne. Early hours, a frugal table, a solitary life; monotony, almost, of pursuits, consisting of a
regular round of official audiences, fixed for each day, and
almost each hour, and unrelieved by court festivities or public recreation—such is the life, more or less, of every
successive Pope. He is not exempt from any of the obligations of his priesthood. He celebrates mass each morning,
and assists at the second celebration. He recites the bre-
viary, like any of his poorest curates; his beads too, most
certainly, like any simple catholic at home or abroad;
besides, probably, other special devotions. He listens to sermons; not merely formal ones in his chapel, but real honest
preachings, strong and bold, by a Capuchin friar, during
Advent and Lent. All this is every-day work; to which must
be added the more public functions in which he takes a

prominent, and often laborious, part. To say that Pius VII lived this life, would be simply to say that he was Pope. Nor would it be an addition, after all that has been stated, to mention that he was kind, considerate, and affable to all around him. But there is one trait in his character which must not be omitted, because it shows the strength of principles acting in opposition to what might have been considered his nature. He set the noble example of "not condescending to flesh and blood." However affectionate his heart might be, it did not lead him to bestow dignity or favour upon his own family. His predecessor, and relation, had unfortunately left a contrary example,—a weakness in a life of strong-minded virtue; a blemish in a pontificate of sorrowful glory. But the seventh Pius, who had renounced family ties, with family comforts, when he entered his noviceship, returned no more to the bonds he had cast aside. He was, in this, irreproachable; and his conduct has been an example and a law to his successors.

This, of course, helped make the isolation of the Pope more complete. Pius VII, however, was in the habit of admitting occasionally into his society, in the evening, a few persons whose conversation he relished. Among these was Canova, the renovator of sculpture, its greatest modern master, and at the same time a noble and virtuous man. Another, who has been mentioned, was his secretary of Latin letters, Monsignor Testa. This excellent man united in himself many rare qualities. He was an elegant classical scholar, and composed his Latin letters as few else could do; he was acquainted with modern languages, which he made use of chiefly for the study of geology and other natural sciences, in which he took great delight. This led to a particular friendship between him and the English College. He was to be found every afternoon taking his walk on Monte Pincio, generally in company with two or three friends, of whom the illustrious Mai was one. There one could join him, and learn the political and ecclesiastical chit-chat of the day. Sometimes a long-bearded Armenian or Syrian, or an American or Chinese missionary, would be in the group, and contribute interesting intelligence from the extremities of the earth. The venerable prelate, who formed the unfailing centre of the society, ever bore a winning smile on his aged countenance, with just the smallest twinkling of drollery,[1] and that sense of the ludicrous which is inseparable from genius, and served to make him suggest questions calculated to bring out any little eccentricities or outlandishness in a narrator. Yet, simple as a child and as warm in his affections, never did an unkind word escape him; nor would he ever take advantage of the canonical exemption which his situation gave him from choral attendance twice a day at Santa Maria Maggiore, of which he was a prebendary.

An anecdote of his early life, related by himself, is interesting, because it refers also to a much more celebrated character. In his youth Testa was attached to the nunciature at Paris, and gained the esteem of many scientific men. Among them was Buffon, who one day asked him to dinner. On entering the drawing-room he found himself unexpectedly in a company composed of the most eminent naturalists and mathematicians of Paris. He was somewhat overawed, though flattered by this attention, when a thought struck him which paralysed his joy and his appetite. It was Friday, a day of abstinence, not much

1. He was one of those priests who refused to take the clergy oath exacted by the French Government, and who were transported to Corsica, and there severely imprisoned. The good people of the neighbourhood used to approach the wall of the fortress where least guarded, and at a favourable moment a basket used to be let down from a barred window, and filled with such comforts as had been provided. Then Monsignor Testa would give the signal from his loop-hole, well known to all captives, of "*Sursum corda*," and the cord was quickly drawn up. When such learned theologians and canonists as Bolgeni and Devoti went astray on the subject of the oath, it required some firmness to refuse it, with the alternative, most trying to a Roman of all persons, of being deported far from Rome. One poor old priest, when told, on refusing the oath, that he should be sent to the island of Corsica, said he had only one request to make—that he might go by land, as the sea would disagree with him.

observed by gentlemen of that class, though his attention or neglect would be narrowly observed. What should he do? How should he manage to play and dabble with forbidden meats, so as to arrive at the end of the meal, hungry but unobserved, and, what was more, unsullied? The doors of the dining room were at length thrown open, but so unhappy was he at his own perplexing situation, that he did not notice the table, till startled by his host's address to his guests: *"Messieurs, aujourd'hui est Vendredi, et il faut l'observer."* He then saw that, evidently in compliment to him, the gentlemen naturalists had to confine their observations to acquatic animals, from whatever other animal reign the cook might have taken his condiments.[1]

In addition to the recreation of occasional evenings in the society of his friends, the Pope invariably took his walk out of the Porta Pia, which was frequented by many who desired thus to obtain his blessing. This was given with the same bland smile to poor as to rich, to the peasant who happened to be driving his donkey loaded with sticks, as to the nobleman who descended from his carriage to kneel on the curbstone. Many a time have the writer and his companions chosen that direction for a walk, and been accosted by a passing salutation full of kindness.

Those, however, who wished to see this Pontiff in his happiest aspect, would follow him to the churches which he might chance to visit; or attend his ecclesiastical functions. His great age, and an accident which he had met with a short time before, prevented him, at the period to which

1. A more unpleasant experience of the same embarassment befell the senator Rezzonico, nephew of Pope Clement XIII. He was on a visit of compliment to Frederick of Prussia, and was invited to dinner on a fast-day, and nothing was provided that he could eat. The king watched, and pressed him with dish after dish, till the senator, seeing his royal host apparently distressed, informed him of the cause of his refusal. The king ordered anything at hand to be got ready, when presently a royal repast of meagre fare was brought in. His fidelity to conscience had been purposely put to the test.

these reminiscences refer, from performing in person any of the greater offices of the Church. His attendance was all that he could give, and that mostly in the palace chapel. Besides at that time he lived exclusively at the Quirinal palace, or Monte Cavallo; so that the solemn and almost sublime Sixtine chapel, with its royal hall and subsidiary Pauline chapel, were little seen, except by lovers of art. The Vatican palace was, indeed, rather a collection of museums than a papal residence, till the next pontificate. In the over-light and freshly decorated chapel of Monte Cavallo, therefore, most of the great offices of the Church, excepting those of Easter-tide and SS. Peter and Paul's feast, were performed; shorn indeed of their great splendour, as now witnessed by every tourist. Even on these greater occasions, and when in the Vatican basilica, the Pope simply attended; but that presence gave to all its colour and solemnity. That spirit of piety which his saintly mother had engrafted on a sweet and gentle nature, was impressed upon his countenance and on his figure. Bent down by age and suffering, his attitude seemed that of continued prayer; sitting or standing, as much as kneeling, he struck your eye as the very picture of earnest and unaffected devotion, abstracted from the ceremonial, the state, or the multitude that surrounded him. It was in one great function, particularly, that this effect was most striking.

On the feast of Corpus Christi the great procession of the day is made round the whole square of St. Peter's; the colonnade of which is continued round along the furthest houses, by means of a temporary portico. The beginning of the procession is entering the church of St. Peter, as its last portion is leaving the Sixtine chapel. It is a spectacle growing at every step in interest. Between the seven-deep lines of spectators, no longer northerns, but country people mostly, many of whom appear in the almost oriental costumes of their villages, rich in velvet, embroidery, and bullion, pass in succession the religious corporations, as they are called, of the city; next, the chapters of the many collegiate

churches, and those of the basilicas, preceded by their peculiar canopy-shaped banners, and their most ancient and
precious crosses, dating even from Constantine. Then
comes that noblest hierarchy that surrounds the first See in
the world, partaking, necessarily, of the double function and
character of its possessor,—prelates of various degrees, holding the great offices of state and of the household, judges,
administrators, and councillors. They are followed by bishops of every portion of the Church, arrayed in the episcopal
robes of their various countries, Latins, Greeks, Melchites,
Maronites, Armenians and Copts. To them succeeds the
Sacred College, divided, like a chapter, into deacons and
priests, but with the addition of the still higher order of
bishops. And at the time of which we write, there were
men distinguished by the important post which they occupied in public affairs, and their share in suffering, and their
example of virtuous constancy. Few of those whose names
occur in Cardinal Pacca's memoirs, and in other records of
the time, were, as yet, wanting to surround the good Pope
with the associations of his previous history. Many of them,
including the eminent historian himself, were, in appearance, most venerable; bearing a heavy weight of years on
their spare erect forms; their heads mingling their thin
white locks with their unblemished ermine, in rivalry of its
whiteness; walking with the gait of princes, and speaking
with the grace of virtuous wisdom; and when seated in
order, during a sacred function, looking so calmly dignified,
so placid and noble, that many must on beholding them
have entertained the same thought which crossed the
writer's fancy. It was, that if an artist wished to represent
the Roman senators silently seated in the Forum, when the
soldiers of Brennus[1] entered, paused and knelt, and wor-
shipped, he would with difficulty have found anywhere else
the fittest models for his picture. But here he would have
possessed all: heads, attitude, expression, feeling, in the

1. Leader of the Gauls who occupied Rome in 390 BC.

very national type of the same people; and moreover, the same order, position, and unimpassioned repose, with such flowing robes and richness of colour, as could guide the imagination to the older scene.

Such were the venerable princes, whose names the stranger asked in a whisper as they passed in that procession before him and immediately preceeded the final group of its moving picture. Its base was formed by almost a multitude of attendants, such as, had they been the object at which one could look, would have carried one back three centuries at least. The bright steel armour of the Swiss guards upon party-coloured doublet and hose—the officers' suits being richly damascened in gold—gleamed amid the red damask tunics of bearers, walking symmetrically and unflinchingly under a heavy burden; while the many two-handed swords of the Swiss flamed upwards, parallel with the lofty poles of a rich silver-tissue and embroidered canopy that towered above all, and was carried by persons who deemed it a high honour, and who also wore the quaint costumes of days gone by.

But high in the air, beneath the canopy, and upon the estrade or small platform borne aloft, is the crowning object of the entire procession. Upon a faldstool richly covered stands the golden Monstrance,[1] as it was anciently called in England, that contains the holiest object of Catholic belief and worship; and behind it the Pontiff kneels, with his ample embroidered mantle embracing the faldstool before him. Thus he is borne along, so that all may see and join him in his devotion, wherein he is undisturbed even by the motion required to walk in a procession. No one who ever saw Pope Pius VII in this position will easily forget the picture. The hands firmly and immovably clasped at the bases of the sacred vessel; the head bent down, not in feebleness but in homage; the closed eyes that saw none of the state and magnificence around, but shut out the world from the

1. Used in the exposition of the Blessed Sacrament.

calm and silent meditation within; the noble features so
composed that no expression of human feeling or of earthly
thought could be traced upon, or gathered from, them; the
bare head, scarcely ever uncovered except then,[1] with locks
still dark floating unheeded in the breeze;—these characteristic forms and appearances of a human frame, unmoving
and unwavering as a sculptured figure, might have been
taken as the purest and sublimest symbol of entranced ado-
ration. The swelling chorus of the hymns and psalms before
him evidently did not reach his ear; the smoke of fragrant
incense just beneath him did not soothe his nostrils; the
waves of a multitude, swayed to and fro with the murmur of
a sea, traced not an image on his eyeballs: he was himself
absracted from all that sense could perceive, and was cen-
tred in one thought, in one act of mind, soul and heart, in
one duty of his sublime office, one privilege of his supreme
commission. He felt, and was, and you knew him to be,
what Moses was on the mountain—face to face, for all the
people, with God; the vicar, with *his* Supreme Pontiff; the
chief shepherd, with the Prince of pastors; the highest and
first of living men, with the One living God.[2]

I record impressions—impressions never to be effaced. It
may be that youth, by its warmth, softens more the mould in
which they are made, so that they sink deeper, and are produced at the same time more sharply and definitely; but
certainly those earlier pictures remain in the memory as the
standard types of what has been seen many times again. When
we have gazed upon many repetitions of a painting by a great
master, we can hardly divest ourselves of the idea that the first

1. The white skull-cap worn by the Pope is called the *Solideo*, because
taken off in homage only to God.
2. On Good Friday, 1818, an English traveller, Mr Matthias, whom Italians
allow to have written Italian verse like a native, was watching, with great
feeling the Pope, as, bareheaded and unsandaled, he advanced up the chapel
to kiss the cross. Some one whispered to him that this was a piece of supersti-
tion. "Oh, say not so," he exclaimed; "it is affecting and sublime."

we saw must have been the original, the others copies.

If thus far the reader has followed what he may consider unalloyed praise, he may have a right to ask, Where are the shadows that must give relief to the lights of our portrait? Cardinal Pacca, his minister, and companion in his most trying situation, has openly declared what was the flaw, or imperfection that struck him, through all his connection with the Holy Pontiff, and it is the one most usually allied with gentleness and meekness. Irresolution, when left to himself, strongly contrasted with courage when, under advice, he clearly saw his duty. Some attributed this failing to the low estimate which the Holy Father had formed of his own abilities—to an habitual humility of thought. No doubt, in his unselfish and simple heart, a failing like this, that easily leans towards virtue's side, naturally took this form; and a poor estimation of his own gifts would both clothe and strengthen a true feebleness that existed. But the fault, if natural, was not one to be cured by the training which matured his other good qualities. There is not, indeed, a happier life for the weak in spirit than that in a community. It most truly relieves the mind of daily and worrying cares, and leaves it serene for occupations that soften and soothe it; but it blunts the edge of that self-reliance, which would cut a knot or thrust aside an obstacle, and it renders counsel easy and accessible, or even indispensable; for where many live together in peaceful community of interests, there is little that requires solitary action. Solitary action would be simply obstructive or disturbing.

The government of the Pope was vigorous and decided, because he knew better than most princes how to choose his minister, and, once chosen, how to give him his confidence. If this work were a history, it would be easy to give proof of this truly sovereign instinct. It may be sufficient to say, that no one could have served him more wisely, at the critical moment when his misfortunes commenced, than their historian, Cardinal Pacca; none could have guided the helm of his shattered vessel more skilfully or more firmly

than the great statesman Consalvi. It was in that middle
space between these two ministers,—when no longer,
indeed, a monarch, but a captive; when bereft of all advice
and sympathy, but closely pressed on by those who, probably themselves deceived, thoroughly deceived him,—that
he committed the one error of his life and pontificate, in
1813. For there came to him men "of the seed of Aaron,"
who could not be expected to mislead him: themselves free
and moving amidst the busiest of the world, they showed
him, through the loopholes of his prison, that world from
which he was shut out, as agitated on its surface, and to its
lowest depths, through *his* unbendingness; the Church as
torn to schism, and religion as weakened to destruction, by
what they termed *his* obstinacy. He who had but prayed and
bent his neck to suffering, was made to appear in his own
eyes a harsh and cruel master, who would rather see all per-
ish, than loose his grasp on unrelenting, but impotent,
jurisdiction.[1]

He yielded in a moment of conscientious alarm; under
false, but virtuous, impressions, he consented, though con-
ditionally, to the terms proposed to him for a new
Concordat. But no sooner had his upright and humble
mind discovered the error, than it nobly and successfully
repaired it. He would have no help from others in this
work, he suffered no man to risk peace or comfort by assisting him. He would be his own secretary; wrote, corrected,
and transcribed the necessary documents; by his humble
candour recovered his bright serenity, his sweet smile, and
unruffled peace; and rose higher in the esteem and love of
all who knew him, from the depth of the self-abasement
into which he nobly descended.

The history of this transaction has long been before the
public under two very different aspects; as related with pas-
sionless simplicity by Cardinal Pacca, or as dramatically and
caustically narrated by the Abbé de Pradt. The one bears all

1. The deputation of bishops and others, who visited him at Savona.

the marks of a sincere recorder of the facts; the other the stamp of a bitter, though witty and clever, partisan. But it is difficult to look back upon the momentous crisis to which we have alluded in the fortunes of the Pope, and, according to mere human calculation, in those of the Church, without a moment's reflection on what forms its highest view.

When, through our own progress, historical events have so far receded from our sight that we no longer dis-cern their lesser details, or the feelings which they excited, they pass into the domain of providential records. The actors in them stand in a more solemn light; their relative proportions, perhaps their place, change; their influence on the world can be measured by results. This is the case even in daily life. The man who first pressed the lever of the printing-press wielded a more powerful and noble sceptre than the sovereign who may have dropped a few coins in his hand as a brave mechanic. Lunardi, who swelled and puffed himself out as much as his balloon, and was admired and honoured by great ones, has passed out of sight, borne away on the very wings of unsubstantial uselessness; while a man who was silently watching at home the vapour from the cauldron, was distilling from it, in the alembic of his brain, a subtler spirit still; for it was to become the very spirit of a coming world.

But when we look back at public men and things placed in the very midst of eventful currents, which flow on, but which they modify, direct, and control irresistibly, they are manfestly not accidents, but causes—now seen and felt to be such—of what moves around them; them-selves subservient to a higher cause. They may allow the stream to flow quietly on one side, and force it to writhe and twist itself on the other; they may be dashed over by a gathering torrent in what before was but a freshet; nay, they may be toppled over, borne down, carried away, and clean dissolved; but to the last they will have been the necessary quantities by which every ordinary law of motion, of pressure, of relative existence has to be modified or estimated. In history the world runs smooth for a time; but the appearance, suddenly in the midst of the stream, of an Alexander, or a Charlemagne, or a Christopher Columbus, destroys the equilibrium of existing forces, by arms, by wisdom, or by a sublimer gift, and prepares a new phase of society, the full value, or importance at least, of which may not be estimable for many generations to come. With all their vices, blunders, crimes, follies, grandeur, and littlenesses, we see in them the instruments of an unusual, stark and strong, providential interposition, beneficient in the end, though sometimes awfully judicial in the beginning.

Into the list of such historical names, short as it is, and severely exclusive, it is impossible not to insert that of Napoleon I. Never was symbol better chosen by a monarch than the eagle was by him. Eagle in his eye, eagle in his soar, eagle in his strength of wing when balanced above his aim, and in swiftness when darting on it; eagle in his gripe; yet eagle in all that distinguishes the king of birds from vulture, hawk or gentle falcon. A warrior by nature, and a conqueror by instinct, with all the roughness of the one, and all the haughtiness of the other; yet fitting a throne as if he had been nursed upon it; surrounding it with the splendour of feudal monarchies, and filling it with the grace of ancient kings; he seemed to have learnt intuitively, in the stern occupations of war, the tastes, the tact, the amenities, and, what was still more, the duties and exigencies, of an imperial royalty. Art and science, almost shamed and even scared, by cruel examples, from society, raised their heads, and threw their grateful homage at the feet of their reviver; an Augustan age of literature broke forth from the chaos of revolutionary barbarism; its brilliant authors hung their thanks, in verse and prose, upon his armour and his ermine; and manufactures sprang up with a taste and profusion which not only shed new lustre round

his halls from Sèvres and the Gobelins, but made France
more than ever the arbiter of elegance and the dictatress of
fashion. To this must be added, the wonderful and inborn
mastership in the craft of government, which he at once
displayed;—his power of domestic organization and internal
rule, whereby he held in his own hands the threads of command, from every department, prefectship and mayorality,
almost as completely if not as instantaneously acting as the
telegraph wire in the cabinet of his present illustrious successor.[1] And, further, add the mental clearness and practical
thinking power required to enable a man to be a lawgiver,
and to draw up a code of universal justice, civil and crimi-
nal, theoretical and applied;—classification of offences,
procedure, adjustment of punishment, prevention, pursuit,
and correction. Such a code, too, as could, and did suit a
people whose cumbersome legislation, "ordonances," *octrois*,
decrees of extinct parliaments, had been swept away by a
ruthless revolution: a people which had acquired new
thoughts, new feelings, new claims; though not new tradi-
tions and usages, to lend either a base or buttress to a legal
system. To have given a body of useful laws had obtained
for Solon and Alonzo, the epithet of the Wise, for Charlemagne that of the Great, for our Edward that of the Good.
And much counsel from practical and studious men, no
doubt, had each one of these singular rulers; there was
much to be compiled, much to be compared, much to be
adjusted to its resting-point by the balance of dissenting or
diverging views. But we have seen how little commissions
for codifying can do, where any amount and extent of pro-
fessional ability and experience are collected, without the
direction and supervision of a master-mind which brings
higher controlling elements into the combination, superior
to technicalites, "wise saws, and modern instances." And

1. Napoleon III had become Emperor of France in 1852 four years before
the publication of these recollections; he was the nephew of Napoleon I.
He was deposed in 1871 after the defeat of France by Prussia in 1870.

therefore the simple title of "Code Napoleon," while it denies no praise to the learned and industrious men who arranged and composed it, tells the future as the present age, who it was that watched over the great work to maturity, presided personally over the deliberations of its compilers, ruled their differences, threw in the valuable ingredient of a strong unbiassed sense; and, if he sometimes embroiled, oftener conciliated, jarring sentiments. Nor is it slender praise of this undertaking, accomplished amidst innumerable other cares, that it should have remained established in countries from which every other vestige of French dominion has vanished;—preserved as of great value by dynasties of rival houses, in spite of the first impulse of sudden restorations to abolish every novelty, and the tendency of time to produce something more national.

"*Quot libras in duce summo!*" [1] we may well exclaim; and ask, Was such a man sent on the public stage without a part allotted to him of supreme importance and inevitable influence? But now another evidence of a providential destiny has come after many years, before us;—one which baffles many a previous calculation. He dashed over the world like a meteor; blazed, dazzled, and dropped completely extinct. He was a phenomenon, a comet if you please, that struck its course athwart the quiet planes of regular orbs, whose mutual attractions and counter-attractions had been part of their periodical laws of motion; and swung them, more rudely than usual, from their steady course. But the disturbing brush was over; the eccentric body had flown by, never to return. "Write this man childless,"[2] had become truth, plainly recorded in the world's history. And that history had scarcely begun to acknowledge and extol what was really great in him, or recognise his indispensable place in the

---

1. Juvenal, Satire XI.148: [What would be the weight at which that mighty leader would tip the scales today?] Juvenal is commenting on Hannibal, the Carthaginian leader who invaded Italy.
2. Holy Bible: Jeremias: 22.30.

world: for whose interest was it to do so?

That yet, after all this, almost a generation later, the ostracised, branded, and proscribed name should be found in the same place, bearing after it the same imperial title, annulled, abolished by the congress of Europe,—with every human probability, and many earnest desires, that both may be continued in a lasting dynasty,—is surely strange and unexpected enough to establish a providential dispensation in the history of the first Emperor. It suggests the idea, that whatever he did or intended, that partook of his nobler and higher nature, his genius, his grandeur of mind, and his faith, are to be preserved and even developed, as a legacy of family love alone can be; while the errors and the excesses that have clouded it will ever serve as traditionary lessons, where they can be most accurately appreciated for avoidance.

All this may, no doubt, appear superfluous; for no one who recognises what we may call providential crises in history, will refuse to acknowledge one in the appearance of Napoleon Bonaparte; rising suddenly and straight, like a solid sea-wall, from the revolutionary abyss, and protecting, against that from which it springs, the shaken and shattered earth. And yet the reader must indulge this vein still further, before the writer's view can be made clear.

Europe has experienced many political revolutions, but it has witnessed only one social one. It has been only by invasion and conquest that an entire and ancient royal dynasty has been swept away; every order of rank and nobility abolished; the whole class of the priesthood, and the national religion, with all its institutions, monuments, rites, and usages, annulled by death, confiscation, destruction, or abrogation; the map of the country pulled to pieces, its provinces remodelled under other names; its weights and measures from the ton to the grain, and from the league to the inch, changed in name and proportion; its divisions of time, from the era of its date to the distribution of the year, of its months, and their subdivisions; and finally the total system of government, finance, justice and municipal administration, effaced and produced anew. When the Turks seized on the Byzantine empire they effected exactly such a revolution; and such the Saracens made in Andalusia and Granada. For even they did not change that stubborn element of nationality—language. The Albanian and the Moldavians, the Arab and the Greek, the scattered tribes of the mountains or the sands, retained their mother-tongues.

What is called the French revolution did therefore, for perhaps the only time in the world's history, what only the complete subjugation of a country by a foreign enemy has ever done. It was a volcano, not so much in the violent and burning outburst of hidden fires, frightfully energetic and appalling, as by its covering with its scoriae and ashes the rich soil and teeming produce of civilisation. These will indeed reappear; the surface, new and unnatural, will be abraded by time and storms; and gradually the germs of old life, crushed but not killed, will struggle through, and be green again above the black field.

The terrible upheaving of the subsoils over the surface, consist they of mobs or clubs, mountains or conventions; the triumph of proletarianism over the noble and the sacred, the aristocracy of genius as of birth; the execrable impartiality of wickedness, which could send a Bailly or a Lavoisier to the scaffold as a Danton or a Robespierre; the persevering struggle to destroy whatever was enlightened by education, study, and familiarity with polished literature and elegant society, seemed to lead almost to the very extinction not of civilisation only, but of whatever could again revive it. For there arose too, from that very slime of corruption and brutality, a crop of ferocious genius and prowess, which threatened not only to render the new order of things permanent, but to endow it with power of propagation and extension. It is hard to say whether this giant power was the nation's will or the nation's arm: whether it gave, or followed, an impulse; whether successive leaders,—

as they rose to the surface of that turbid pool, controlled its billows for a while, and then were tossed to be impaled upon its rocks,—forced their way up by innate might, or were pushed and whirled by the turbulence below into the upper air. But, one after the other, they showed no higher or nobler thoughts and aims than the basest and most sanguinary of those who had upheaved them; no more instinct for morality, order, or civilisation, no more reverence for genius or virtue, no more desire to turn the flow of social energies into their usual channels, and regain the calm breath and steady pulse that alone are evidence of national vitality. For this they mistook the tremendous outbreaks of rude strength, and the choking throbs of maniacal access.

Count de Maistre, with truthful humour, describes the human animal as composed of three elements, soul, body, and—*bête*.[1] When the bestial element gets the uppermost, it must be for a wild start and headlong career of some sort; and here it was for a wild political debauch. The people, as it was called, had plunged, and reared, struggled, and wrenched itself loose from whatever it considered a load to which it had been unjustly yoked; whether the wain of laborious industry, or the golden car of royal state. In doing this, it had torn every tie which connected it with social order. It had broken "the triple cord" of the domestic charities; for often the greatest enemies of a man were those of his own house.[2] It had snapped the golden chain of mutual interest which united different classes, till, after reckless plunder and systematic confiscation, *assignats* had become the wretched substitute for coin. In fine, it had even rent the tougher thongs, by which justice binds and scourges delinquent members of society; for revolutionary tribunals had taken the place of the calm judgment-seat; or rather it

1. *Voyage autour de ma Chambre*.
2. A few years ago, after the barricades, a number of prolétaires, left destitute in Paris, whither they had come to find work or plunder, were kindly provided with food and lodging in a college; where also pains were taken to give them some moral instruction. All seemed becomingly

was a more terrible procedure, by mob accusation, trial and sentence, and execution.

One band only remained unbroken, flung loose upon the neck, in its wild career; and he who should have courage enought to seize it, and cool prudence to handle it, so as to wheel round almost unconsciously, and bring back to the beaten track of nations, this yet uncontrollable energy, would, indeed, be the man of his age, and the retriever of his country. This rein which no Phaethon could have seized without being dashed, as many had been, to pieces, was the intense love of country; a love like all else near it, passionate, fierce, and scorching; that burnt for vengeance on every foe, scorned the opposition of the entire world, was darkly jealous of every glory gained for it by every king, though it turned itself into hatred at the very name. There can only be one man at a time equal to such an emergency; and looking back after fifty or sixty years, no one can doubt that a higher will than man's, a better cause than fate, gave him his destiny.

He snatched, in the right moment, this only rein which could guide back his country to the beaten way; seconding its last noble impulse, he gained his mastery over it, soothed it, caressed it; then called into action once more the dormant instincts of classified society, subordination, moral responsibility, and at last religion. The opportune appearance of such a man, gifted with such a combination of

accepted, when the superior, hoping to soften still more their minds and hearts, showed to some of them the stains of blood which still marked the floor, from the massacres of the great revolution. One of the men, after listening to his account, exclaimed: "Ah, Monsieur! vous ne nous connaisez pas. Nous ferions autant. Nous sommes del la boue nous autres. Nous accepterions votre pain avec une main, nous vous poignarderions avec l'autre." [Ah, sir, you don't know us. We would do as much again. We ourselves are from the gutter. We would accept your bread with one hand, and stab you with the other.] Has the reader ever met a crowd coming away from an execution? Has he ever seen another like it? Where did it come from? Similar questions used to be asked at Paris in the days of the terror, and used to be answered with almost a superstitious shudder.

necessary qualifications, as indispensable then as at all times rare, becomes, so contemplated, a providential fact.

This consideration does not oblige or lead us to approbation of a single act against justice, religion, or truth. Not one aggressive war, not one deed of oppression, however brilliant in its execution or plausible in its motives; not one act of spoliation or violence, or irreverence to person, place, or thing; nothing, in fine, unjustifiable by the eternal laws of justice, can we, or will we, approve. Every extenuating consideration must have its weight with us; every pleading motive for excuse we leave to a higher tribunal, where judgment is more merciful than man's. It is not a little to say, that a young soldier, formed in such times as his, flattered and spoiled by men and by fortune, should have so earnestly sought and obtained the legitimate restoration of religion, its hierarchy, its influence, and its complete organisation, free from modern theories of doctrine, or foreign systems of government.

And especially nobody will, for a moment, suspect us of wishing to mitigate the guilt of what he himself deplored and repented of,—the treatment of the venerated Pontiff whom we may seem to have forgotten. Although, no doubt, his violent removal from Rome was not commanded by the Emperor; and still less could he have intended the rudeness, irreverence, and sacrilegiousness of the mode in which it was done; yet the injury was not repaired, nor were its sufferings compensated. The responsibility was unhappily assumed, and so incurred. To deplore the fault, is to testify feelings very different from aversion or even anger. It is what one does with the warning offences of a David and a Solomon.

Yes, Providence brought the two together for a great wise purpose. The one, borne away beyond the purposes of his first glorious mission, after he had mastered his noble steed, had allowed it to trample under-foot the nations, and dash its hoof over the necks of princes. Like Cyrus, he had forgotten from whom came his power and strength; and he believed that nothing could resist his might. Not impressed by early education with any clear idea of the marked limits of two powers essentially distinct on earth; ill-advised by those who should have been his counsellors, who, with a single exception,[1] left uncorrected, or rather seconded, the feeling which experience had made a second nature—the very secret of unbroken success—that being irresistible he must not be resisted;—he brought himself into collision where, humanly speaking, he could not doubt of victory. The well-wrought iron vase met in the stream the simple vessel of softest clay. The steel armour of the warrior brushed against the soft texture of the sacerdotal vestment. In either case, which was sure to give way?

We come then to the great moral of this historical, or rather providential, moment. To the catholic mind the reading is simple. It required a man of marvellous genius, of irresistible power, of unfailing success; of singular quickness in measuring opposition, in reading character, in seizing the key to the present position, the passes to the future; a daring master of destiny, a soldier, a chieftain, a law-giver, an emperor in mind and presentiment;—it needed all this and more, to form the man who should subdue the most tremendous social convulsions, and give designation to his era of history. Well, and no wonder he deemed himself invincible! And while he stood on his own ground, sat on his war-steed, or on his throne, he was so.

But there needed only a plain and simple monk, brought up in the cloister, ignorant of the world, single-minded in his aims, guileless and artless in his word and speech, not eloquent, not brilliant in qualities and attainments, meek, gentle, sweet, humble-minded, and devout; it required only a Pope of average character in the qualifications of his state, to prove that there was a power superior to that of a mighty conqueror, and give to the age a rival, though unbelted hero.

And no wonder if the captor was made a captive, and the conqueror subdued. For he had left his own ground, he had dismounted from his charger, he had descended from his

1. Abbé Emery; and Napoleon respected and honoured him for it.

throne:—he had stepped into the sanctuary. And there the old man of mild aspect and gentle voice was in his own.[1] And the whole could only be a repetition of a scene often repeated there; and its result was only the execution of an eternal law.

The Emperor Arcadius, more perhaps through evil counsel than through malice, had the great Bishop St. John Chrysostom removed from his patriarchal see, and carried away into the fastness of cold inclement mountains. Years after his death, Theodosius and Pulcheria made reparation in the same city, publicly and fearlessly, for the injury inflicted on so holy a man.

And has there been virtually no repetition of this same noble and generous scene? Upon how many a French soldier and officer has the splendid statue of Pius in the Vatican seemed to look down, smiling and forgivingly, and with hand outstretched to shed a blessing, at once sacerdotal and paternal?

---

1. We must naturally reject every unauthenticated story of rudeness personally shown to the holy Pontiff. A celebrated interview of Fontainebleau has been made the subject of a picture by an eminent artist (Wilkie); and dramatic accounts have been given of what there passed. The Italian biographer of Pius VII, who published his work two years after the Pope's death in Rome itself, then full of intimate friends, admirers, and companions of his misfortunes, who had heard his own narrative of his sufferings, gives a very different account of the conclusion of this interview from that generally reported; and he is by no means disposed to partiality in favour of the Emperor. After giving a description of a conversation, animated on both sides, and carried on in so loud a tone as to resound through the neighbouring rooms, he related in full the Pope's calm summary of all that he had done and suffered for the preservation of the Church and of religion. It ended by a firm but mild expression of his determination to undergo anything rather than consent to what was demanded. He continues:—"Napoleon, who had listened attentively, was moved by his firmness of purpose, joined to such an apostolic simplicity. He was calmed, embraced the Pope, and, on leaving, said, 'Had I been in your place, I would have done the same.' " (Pistolesi, vol.iii. p.142.) Was not this taking the captor captive, and subduing in the noblest sense? And what more honourable homage could have been paid to the conduct of the Pope?

CHAPTER V

CONDITION AND FEELINGS OF ROME

A T the period to which the foregoing chapters relate, it was not difficult to learn the feelings with which every class in Rome looked back at the time through which the country had lately passed, and those with which the people contemplated their actual condition.

The Romans, whatever changes may have occurred in their character, have always retained, as an inalienable part of their inheritance, a sensitive consciousness that their city can hold no secondary rank. In every vicissitude of fortune this has been the law of her existence. The translation of the empire to Constantinople, or of the kingdom of Italy to Ravenna, or of the papal court to Avignon, might have appeared sufficient to strip her of her rank; while the succesive spoliations, sackings, burnings, and demolitions, inflicted by barbarians or factions, would have accounted for her sinking to the position of Veii or Collatium. But the destiny of Rome had risen above every catastrophe, superior to all accidents, and to all designs hostile to her supremacy. Now, for the first time, Rome had been but a provincial city, subject to a foreign dominion, governed by a military chief, with a new municipal and judicial system, and a total change in social relations. Even the computation of time was altered. The peace-nurtured children of the soil were subjected to military conscription, which rent them from their families, and sent them far away to the frozen regions of Russia, or the torrid shores of Andalusia, to bleed and die for strangers.

From many causes, the population of Rome had dwindled by the year of the occupation, till from 153,000 it had been reduced to 117,000;[1] many of the best families had left it, some indeed to occupy posts of trust in other portions of the Empire, others to escape the responsibilities and honours of a government towards which they felt no attraction. Money had become scarce; the abundant sources of public and private charity had been dried up; assignats had first been freely circulated, and then suddenly made valueless; and many honest families had been driven to want.[2]

The sweeping away of the Court, with its many dependencies, the breaking up of the households of perhaps fifty cardinals, and of many prelates and ambassadors, had thrown thousands out of direct employment, and tens of thousands of workmen, artists and artisans, to whom such establishments gave occupation. At the same time were necessarily closed the various offices for the administration of ecclesiastical affairs, local and general, which gave bread to more laymen than clerks.

Another and a sensitive sore in the minds of the Romans had been the loss of so many objects, which elsewhere might be things of luxury, but in Rome were almost necessaries of life. The most precious manuscripts of the Vatican, with which they were by various names associated (*Codex Vaticanus* was a title of honour), the invaluable collection of medals, every statue and group of fame, the masterpieces of painting in all the churches, the archives

1. The first was the population in 1800; the second in 1813. This was the minimum. There was a steady increase till 1837, when the cholera augmented the deaths from 3,000 to 12,000. Between 1848 and 1849 the population diminished by 13,000. On the return of the present Pope (Pius IX) it again increased, and last year (1857) it had reached 178,798.

2. A gentleman of great credit informed me that, going out one morning early, he saw standing, among many others, a nobleman awaiting the opening of a baker's shop, that he might buy bread which had to be the sustenance of his family for the day. He had no servant to send; and he entreated my informant not to tell any one of his having seen him in so painful a situation.

of the Vatican and of other departments of ecclesiastical government, and many other treasures, to Rome invaluable, had been removed. The noble halls of the Vatican and Capitol had been empty and deserted: for plaster casts, and a few artists obliged to be content with them, could ill replace the original marbles, and the crowds that used to flock to admire them. Private galleries had shared a similar fate. The Borghese collection of statues had been sold to the Emperor; and the Albani museum had been in part removed, but fortunately was in part only packed up for the journey, and thus to a great extent saved.[1]

If Rome had deplored, and most justly, the loss of her arts, her greatest secular ornaments, what must have been her grief at the religious desolation into which she had been plunged? For to the letter almost it might have been said, that "her streets had mourned, because no one came any longer to her solemn festivals." The crowds of strangers who yearly visit Rome will acknowledge, that it is not merely for the sake of her unrivalled monuments that they travel so

1. The collection of antiquities in the Borghese villa, 255 in number, including the monuments of Gabii, were bought in 1808 by the Emperor, and paid for according to contract. The sale may be considered a forced one; though, in truth, fear of an English invasion was the only real constraint. For the Emperor had negotiated in vain with his brother-in-law, the Prince, up to that period. The sale was made under protest from the Government, as it was contrary to law. In 1814, the family claimed back its antiquities; but Louis XVIII refused to part with them, as lawfully purchased.

The case of the Albani collection was more severe. In 1798 the French Directory confiscated the whole Albani property, as well as that of the Braschi family. The magnificent Albani villa, near Rome, was stripped of its sculptures and marbles, and these, with books and paintings of the house, were sent to Paris. Only a few cases, that were lying in the Roman custom-house in 1802, were then restored. In 1814, the Cardinal Joseph Albani, backed by the Austrian and Roman governments, demanded restitution of the family property. Although allied to the House of Austria by blood, the family had been suffering distress from the confiscation. On the 9th of October, 1815, the celebrated relief of

far, but that the religious ceremonies, which they expect to witness, form no small portion of their attraction. Why else do all flock to Naples during the weeks that intervene between those celebrations, and abandon its early spring, its transparent sea and golden orange-groves, just at the moment when Rome is stripped of everything cheerful, its very bells are hushed, and its music consists of lamentations and *misereres?*

Rome is a city of churches, neither more nor less than a city of galleries and museums: for its churches enter into this class of wonders too. Architecture, painting, sculpture, rich marbles, metal-work, decoration, artistic effects of every sort, are to be found, separate or combined, in the churches. Many are grand in their outlines, though poor in detail, while others present no great features, yet are teeming with artistic treasure. Here is a fresco by Raffaele, there a chapel or a group by Michelangelo; in this is a dome by Lanfranco, in that spandrils by Domenichino; in one a mass of unique marble, a huge flight of steps of materials sold elswhere by the ounce; in another a gorgeous altar of precious stones enshrining a silver statue. But I well remember old men who wept when you spoke of these things; as the sires of Israel did, who could contrast the new temple of Jerusalem with the vanished glories of the old. Everything was now poor, compared with what they had seen before the Treaty of Tolentino,[1] and the subsequent levies of

Antinous was restored to Sig. Santi, the Cardinal's commissioner; and in December following, the remaining pieces of sculpture from his museum, thirty-nine in number, were purchased for the Louvre by Louis VIII. Among these are the beautiful statue of Euripides, another Antinous as Hercules, equally valuable, with several precious busts. Of the pictures and books, and of many other pieces of glyptic art, no account was ever had, as far as we have heard.

1. Signed on the 19th of February 1797 between Bonaparte and the Papacy. By this Pius VI renounced papal rights to Avignon & Bologna, undertook to pay 30 million livres to France, to grant the French Republic 100 works of art, to close Papacy ports to ships of countries at war with France, and to free all Jacobins. Bonaparte in turn agreed to remove his troops from papal lands.

church treasure during foreign occupation.

However, even all this was but secondary to the greater loss of persons compared with things. Many of the churches of Rome are built for large bodies of clergy to serve them; and these had disappeared. Then came the still more irreparable loss of a sovereign priest (like Melchisedec) officiating before and for his people; with his ministers of state, his high princes and nobles surrounding and assisting him, bringing to the service of God what elsewhere is royal state. Such a ceremonial had its own proportioned seats, in the greater basilicas, never seen as they deserve to be, at other times. St. Peter's, else, is a grand aggregation of splendid churches, chapels, tombs, and works of art. Thus it becomes a whole, a single, peerless temple, such as the world never saw before. That central pile, with its canopy of bronze as lofty as the Farnese palace, with its deep-diving-stairs leading to a court walled and paved with precious stones, that yet seems only a vestibule to some cavern of a catacomb, with its simple altar that disdains ornament in the presence of what is beyond the reach of human price—that which in truth forms the heart of the great body, placed just where the heart should be,—is only on such occasions animated, and surrounded on every side, by living and moving sumptuousness. The immense cupola above it ceases to be a dome over a sepulchre, and becomes a canopy above an altar; the quiet tomb beneath is changed into the shrine of relics below the place of sacrifice—the saints under the altar;—the quiet spot at which a few devout worshippers at most times may be found, bowing under the one hundred lamps, is crowded by rising groups, beginning from the lowest step, increasing in dignity and richness of sacred robes; till, at the summit and in the centre, stands supreme the Pontiff himself, on the very spot which becomes him, the one living link in a chain, of which the very first ring is riveted to the shrine of the apostles below.

This position no one else can occupy, with any associations that give it its singular character. It is only his presence that puts everything there in its proper place, and combines all the parts into a significant unity. St. Peter's is only itself, when the Pope is at its high altar; and hence only by, or for, him is it ever used.

All this of course had ceased to be: it was a plain impossibility to attempt any substitution for it. It might be said, that the highest form of religious celebration known in the Catholic Church, as indeed in the Christian world, had been abolished, or suspended without intention of its being ever resumed. It was impossible for a people, so proud of the spiritual preeminence of its ecclesiastical government, and of the grandeur with which this was exhibited on solemn occasions, not to feel all the mortification and abasement involved in this privation.

There can be no difficulty, therefore, in imagining that the restoration of the Pontifical Government had been hailed, and at the time of which we write, was still regarded as a return to happiness and prosperity, as a passage from gloom and sullenness to brightest cheerfulness. And so, at that time, everyone spoke. No doubt the seeds of other thoughts had been left in the ground, by those who had so long held them. It will always happen that some profit more under an unlawful tenure than under a legitimate master; and it had always been noticed, that in every measure of spoliation and violence, not only was the necessary information furnished, but the most disloyal part was taken, by natives and subjects. But these, and other like them, must be considered as, then at least, exceptions. The many who had experienced

> ..."Come sa di sale
> Il pane altrui, e come è duro calle
> Lo scendere a il salir per le altrui scale,"[1]

the nobles, that is, who, of blood scarcely less than royal and even imperial, had been obliged to pay court to strangers of much lower rank, and indeed to solicit their

1. Dante La Divina Commedia: Paradiso, XVII: 58-9. [knowing the taste of the salt in another's bread, and how hard it is to trundle up and down another's staircase,]

patronage; the merchant class who had suffered from general stagnation; and the peasantry, whose traditional loyalty had always been seasoned with religious reverence, were here of one mind. With more general truth than when the words were first written, we may say that, on Pius the Seventh's return, "Italy changed her mourning attire."[1] Not only the artist, but the homeliest citizen of Rome, rejoiced, as he saw the huge cases pass along the street, which he was told contained the Laocoon or Apollo, the Transfiguration or the Communion of St. Jerome. And even objects of minor interest to many, the manuscripts of the Vatican, the archives of the Palace, of the public ministries, even of the Holy Office, were welcomed back with joy, as evidence of a return to what everyone considered the normal state.

And so when, upon his return to Rome, Pius VII proceeded for the first time, after many years, to the balcony in the porch of the Vatican basilica, to pronounce once more his solemn benediction over the assembled crowds, not only of Rome, but of its neighbouring towns and surrounding territory, the commotion of all was, beyond description, tender. To many still young this was the first occasion of witnessing a scene never to be forgotten. As within the church, all may be said to have been arranged and almost predestined for the function at the great pontifical altar, so, outside, one would suppose that everything was accessory to the papal benediction. On any other day, the great square basks in the mid-day sun with unalluring magnificence. Its tall obelisk sends but a slim shadow to travel round the oval plane, like the gnomon of a huge dial; its fountains murmur with a delicious dreaminess, sending up massive jets like blocks of crystal into the hot sunshine, and receiving back a broken spray on which sits serene an unbroken iris, but present no "cool grot" where one may enjoy their freshness; and, neglecting the shorter path, the pilgrim looks with dismay at the dazzling pavement and long flight of unsheltered

1. *Ad ejus reditum lugubres vestes Italia mutavit*. St. Jerome.

steps between himself and the church, and prudently plunges into the forest of columns at either side of the piazza, and threads his way through their uniting shadows, intended, as an inscription tells him, for the express purpose;[1] and thus sacrifices, to the comfort of a cooler approach, the view of the great church, towards which he has perhaps been wending his way for days.

But on the days that the sovereign Pontiff bestows his blessing from the *loggia* as it is called, that is, from above the principal entrance to the portico of the church, no one thinks of the heat, or sultriness even, of the day, aggravated though it be by the crowd of many thousand panting bodies. Everything seems arranged for one purpose: and no other place on earth could answer half so well. The gigantic flights of steps leading to the church, with immense terraces between, are covered with such a carpet as no loom ever wove. Groups of peasantry from the neighbouring towns and villages cover it; some standing in eager expectation, many, chiefly women and children, stretched at full length, waiting more calmly. The men are in their gayest attire, with blue or green velvet jackets, their hair gathered in a green silk net, with white stockings; and such silver buckles at the knee, and still more on the foot, that if such articles had been discovered in an ancient tomb, and supposed to give a rule of proportion for the primaeval wearer, they would have given the lie to the old proverb: "*ex pede Herculem.*"[2] But the female attire on those occasions, far more than now, since the invasion of Manchester has reached even Appenine villages, was characteristically distinct. The peasants of Frascati and Albano, with immense gold earrings and necklaces, the silver skewer through the hair under snow-white flat kerchief, with richly

1. The inscription is from the Holy Bible: Isaias: 4.6: "A tabernacle for a shade in the daytime from the heat, and for a security and covert from the whirlwind and from rain."
2. [By his foot you can recognise Hercules.]

brocaded stomachers and showy silks, looked almost poor beside the oriental splendour of the costume, supposed to be in truth Saracenic, of the dames from Nettuno. A veil of domestic texture of gold, relieved by stripes of the richest colours, formed the crown of a dress truly elegant and magnificent. Gay colours also form the predominant feature of more inland districts, as of Sonnino and Sezze.

Such a multitude covers the steps and terraces, and converts them into a living parterre, masses of bright colour waving to and fro, as in the breeze. Below on the level ground are ranges of equipages filled wiith more aristocratic visitors; and further still there is an open military square, in the middle of which a brilliant staff glitters in the sun. The embacing arms of the elliptical colonnade, expanding and reentering, seem with ease to hold within their margin the vast assembly; and the dark shadowy spaces between the pillars are relieved by glimpses of golden state carriages, and the nodding heads of plumed horses enjoying the cool retreat.

So rich and varied, and yet harmonious, a scene could be produced by one person only, and for a single and almost momentary act. For hours the more patient and devout, who want nothing else, have been basking and melting in the sun; and for some time the more eager have been rushing from every direction to reach the preappointed place of sight. The bell has been tolling a heavy monotonous boom; its sudden hush is a signal for that indescribable, tide-like murmur, and inarticulate heave, which in a crowd implies silence. Every eye is turned to one point: in that instant every person and every thing is in its own proper place: no lens has a focus more accurate, or more powerfully concentrates its rays, than the space over the central balcony, just large enough to contain one human countenance, which was lately blank but is now filled up. By whatever feeling the eye may be directed; by the simple faith of the Italian, the love of picturesqueness of the German, the curiosity of the unbeliever, or the cynicism of the Exeter Hall declaimer;— each is inevitably turned, however reluctantly, to that one point; fifty thousand eyes are concentrated upon one aged man's face; and in the look of the good old man there is holy fascination that keeps them spell-bound for the few moments that he is before them; they can look at nothing else. And what is the purpose of all this?

It is the vision of a moment. After long expectation, a few heads are just seen, hardly recognisable, above the balustrade of the balcony; then the *flabellae* or fans of state; and last, lifted high, the mitred pontiff. A few words are spoken, which are undistinguishable to the crowd beneath. The Pope rises, raises to heaven his eyes, opens wide his arms, and pours out from a full heart, and often with a clear sonorous voice, a blessing on all below. Amidst the clang of bells, the clatter of drums, and the crash of military bands, while the trumpet is yet speaking to the cannoneer, and he to heaven, the vision has departed: the observed of all observers seems to have melted from before the eye, which finds itself gazing once more on vacancy. The father is gone, but has left his blessing to his loving children. Can a position so preeminent be allotted to any other human being? Could another sovereign periodically become the centre of anything so magnificent, morally as well as materially? Could he bring together thousands of strangers and of subjects, ambassadors, kings, and even emperors, with multitudes of poor, who would make pilgrimage on foot from distant regions, and collect them on a single spot, that they might look up to him, for a few moments, or even fall on their knees, as he showed himself at a window of his palace?

Yet who has ever witnessed the papal benediction of St Peter's, and pronounced or felt it to contain a single particle of the ridiculous in it? Or, rather, who has ever thought it less than sublime? And on what rests the difference? On an irresistible belief that no earthly elevation gives a power to bless; that such a power is inherent in the highest degree in only one man; and that the possession of that single power makes it worth while for the greatest and the least to come any distance to partake, if they believe; if not, at least to be spectators of its marvellous exercise. Certainly all will agree, that, if it do exist, it could not possibly be used more gloriously, or in a manner more worthy of it. An improvement on this is hardly imaginable; never did a great occasion so completely create its own circumstances.

If the recollection of a scene so well remembered, because so often witnessed, and generally from the midst of the peasants' position, has carried the writer away from his real subject, he returns by remarking, how enhanced must the exciting and moving ceremonial of the Pope's blessing have been, in its association with his restoration. It wanted, no doubt, the more dignified and colder attendance of foreign visitors; there were not so many handsome equipages glancing in the sun; but their places were filled up by the tens of thousands more of fervent subjects, who had poured in from greater distances than usual, to welcome their sovereign and Pontiff. It was at this function, more than in any other portion of his triumphal procession, that the gush of spontaneous emotion became irresistible, and consequently universal; so as to leave no eye tearless, and no heart unmoved.

There can be no reason to doubt the sincerity of these feelings; and that the people in the widest sense of the word rejoiced at the restoration of a native, though an ecclesiastical, government. Indeed this peculiarity was to them a chief recommendation. It had been to them, in their youth, a kind, paternal, and peaceful rule, and they who were too young to remember it, had received their ideas of it from parents and masters, then deploring the changes which they had experienced. It cannot be unfair or unreasonable to appeal to those who had tried a variety, for a rational opinion as to a preference. A generation has intervened since those days of bitter recollection, during which, no doubt, much has been forgotten of family sorrows and public decline; the love of change and passion for novelty, which are inherent in youth, and form indeed phases of its characteristic feeling of hope, are strong enough to counteract the pleadings of experience, and give reality in the imagination to specious promises of an untested future.

In proof of these assertions we may observe, that when, in 1821, Naples was disturbed by a revolution that overthrew the throne, inflammatory proclamations were spread through the papal dominions, calling on the people to rise and join the four revolutionary camps at Pesaro, Macerata, Spoleto, and Frosinone. Cardinal Consalvi, in the name of the Pope, issued a proclamation, in which he merely reminded the people of their past experience, expressing his assurance that a word would suffice to secure them against the evil intentions of traitors. He bade them remember "how chimerical and deceitful, in past attempts to overthrow social order, had been the prospects held out of an imaginary happiness; how false the promises to protect religion and recompense virtue; how frail and delusive the assurance of a better administration of justice, of greater liberty, of a diminution of imposts, and increase of salaries." And he expressed all confidence, that these reminiscences and experiences would be sufficient antidote against seditious and rebellious attempts.

Nor was he deceived. The storm passed by harmless; no rising took place; and the people showed how the appeal to experience came home to their convictions.

CHAPTER VI

CARDINAL CONSALVI

I T is impossible to treat of the latter portion of this Pontificate, especially to make any allusion to the principles of its government, without bringing before the reader's notice the man whose figure mingles with every reminiscence of the period, and who was the very spring and regulator of the entire policy which distinguished it. This was Hercules Consalvi, the prime minister of Pius from his restoration till his death.

He was born in 1756, and consequently had received his education long before the symptoms of what afterwards convulsed Europe had fairly manifested themselves. Early impressions are usually so deep as not to be effaced by subsequent ones; and it is possible that the partiality which Consalvi always manifested towards England, in his political career, may be traceable to the early kindness and favour which he received from one who always considered and called himself an Englishman. The last of the Stuarts, the amiable and beneficent Cardinal Henry, or the Duke of York, was bishop of Frascati, and would never exchange his see for those borne by the Dean and Subdean of the Sacred College. Of that prettily-situated city, successor of Tusculum, from which the bishop yet derives his title, the Cardinal is still considered the great benefactor. Whatever else may have been wanting for his title, to a royal heart he was no pretender. His charities were without bounds; poverty and distress were unknown in his see. The episcopal palace was almost, if not entirely, rebuilt by him, though he generally resided in a neighbouring villa; the cathedral was much improved and richly furnished. But the seminary, or diocesan ecclesiastical College, was the object of his peculiar care.[1]

1. The diocese of Frascati was full, when the author first knew it, of recollections of the Cardinal Duke, all demonstrative of his singular goodness and simplicity of character. He was accessible to the innocent flattery paid by recognition of his rank: it is recorded of the late Duke of Sussex, that he generously addressed him by the title which he loved, that of "Royal Highness." One is so used to hear little that is good of the Fourth George, that it is pleasing to remember how, in the days of the excellent Cardinal's old age and distress, by loss of his pensions and benefices through the French invasion, the Prince offered him a pension, which was gratefully accepted; and afterwards gave Canova the commission for the Stuart monument—not the happiest production of his chisel—the erection of which in St. Peter's the writer well remembers. The Cardinal

Most of it was built by him, and the library, a most elegant apartment, and rich in many English works, was the fruit of his munificence. Though he was not himself either learned or endowed with great abilities, he knew the value of learning and abilities, engaged excellent professors for his seminary, and brought men of genius round him. Hence his college was frequented not only by aspirants to the clerical state, but by youths of the best families, destined for secular professions.

Among these was the young Roman Ercole, or Hercules, Consalvi. There he distinguished himself, and at some public exhibition, caught the eye of the Cardinal bishop, who honoured it, according to custom, with his presence. Let not the reader be startled if he hears that it was rather by the ornamental than by the useful arts that the future statesman captivated the good Duke-bishop's affections. It is said to have been this skill and grace in a musical performance that first attracted his notice.

Be this as it may, it appears that the young man himself was favoured early with one of those presentiments of future destiny which are the privilege of genius. He possessed, while yet a boy in college, that latent consciousness of power, of energy, and of perseverance, which creates success;

always spoke highly and kindly of the reigning family. He left endowments for the education of ecclesiastical students for Scotland.

His munificence was extended to other objects. Being arch-priest of St. Peter's he presented that basilica with a splendid gold chalice, encrusted with the jewels of the Sobieski family; and this, being still kept in his house when the treasury of the church was plundered, escaped the spoliation, and, till three years ago, was used at the great pontifical celebrations at St. Peter's.

One more anecdote may find a place here, related by one who knew him well. When he first came to Rome, so ignorant was he of the value of coins, that once, on having been shown some place or object of curiosity, he was asked what should be given to the attendant. As he was puzzled, his chamberlain suggested; "Shall I give him a zecchino?" a gold piece, worth 10s. Thinking that the diminutive termination must indicate a small coin, the duke replied, "I think that is too little. Give him a grosso!," a silver 5p.

one may say, speaking profanely, that confidence in one's star—more religiously, that trust in Providence—which encourages to extraordinary efforts a genius otherwise timid and distrustful of itself. Many a gifted mind has pined away, and faded early, from want of this sustaining confidence in a higher direction. But of those who have succeeded in doing anything good for mankind, there can be few who have not experienced early a craving for it, a deep sentiment that they must attempt it, and a strong assurance that they were only to be instruments in higher, and stronger, and better hands, for their appointed work. By some, indolence and pride may be mistaken for this holy consciousness of future power; but the difference of objects proposed will generally give an easy test of the source of either feeling. However, few have the courage to proclaim sentiments which may be so easily mis-attributed; and this the young Consalvi did not hesitate to do. We may imagine that his audience, at one of those annual exhibitions common in all continental colleges, was astonished to hear him openly avow his assurance of future distinction, fame, and wealth. This he did in a poetical composition, which has fortunately been preserved in the library of the Frascati seminary, and deserves to be published here, I believe for the first time.[1]

It is written in the taste of the last century, in that now intolerable allegory, which clothes virtues in the dress of pagan divinities, and personifies, as good or evil beings of another order, the qualities, actions, or sufferings of man. It will also be seen from the title that the young Marquis Consalvi was already a member of Arcadia, the great poetical society of Rome, and bore in consequence a name bucolic, as well as his family designation.

1. Some time before his death, perhaps a year or two, the Cardinal had privately printed a sort of medical autobiography. It was a minute account of his maladies, and the treatment of them by physicians, probably drawn up for consultation. I read it at the time, and remember some curious particulars, but I have not been able to procure a copy.

"DEL SIG^{R.} MARCHESE ERCOLE CONSALVI
FRA GLI ARCADI FLORIDANTE ERMINIANO
SUL RITORNO AI SUOI STUDI

POEMETTO

"ME che riporto alle belle arti, e ai dolci
Industri studj desioso il piede.
E che dal lungo vaneggiar richiamo
Quelle che mille immagini vezzose
E mille idee in un sol punto, e in uno
Momento suol pittrice fantasia
Vaga crear: Pallade amica, e sola
Dolce conforto, e non minor diletto
Di quei, cui porser pargoletto il latte
Le suore che hanno sede in sul Parnasso,
Con lieto squardo caramente accogli:
L'egida poni, e la terribil asta
Onde t'armi la destra, e svegli in petto
Cui delicato cor alto spavento.
Tu cortese qual sei, Tritonia Diva,
Figlia del sommo reggitore de' Numi
Porgimi aita; piano e facil dammi
Questo sentiero, e i voti miei seconda.
Io sovra d' esso affetterò ben ratto
I passi miei, e tergerò pur lieto
Dalla pallida fronte i miei sudori
Se allor che a destra ed a sinistra io volgo
Il guardo, a te mirar, Diva, vedrotti
Oltre l' usato tuo lieta guardarmi,
Con dolci riso sulla rosea bocca,
Con bella grazia alle ridenti ciglia
Un tuo sorriso, od un gentil tuo detto,
Conforterammi il cuor tremante, e a lui

Darà lena bastante. Allor, sì, allor
Vengane pure, il bieco guardo torva
Con quelle scarne sue livide guancie
E con quelle aggrottate orride ciglia
L' indefessa mai sempre aspra fatica,
Non mai stanca in operare, e mi minacci
Lunghe, e fiere vigilie, affanni, e stenti.
Io sì, che sotto la tua scorta, a vile
Terrò listenti, ed ogni duro affanno
Ed ogni angoscia, sprezzerò ben forte
La Donna iniqua, e di costanza armato
E più che smalto invigorito il petto
A giogo la terrò; farolle il torvo
Ciglio abbassar. Sì giungerò là dove
Mi guida dolce amabile desio,
Che di bella speranza esser si pregia
Parto gentil, che via pur troppo al cuore
Mi fa invito, e lusinga. Aspettan, sollo,
Me onor, gloria, ricchezza, al bell' oprare
Sprone, e conforto desiabil. Certo
È questo il fato mio: questa è la tela
Che tra le man del ciel, per me s'intesse,
Ma che? forse sogn' io? e non piuttosto
Sì verace m' inspira amico nume?
Non che non sogno, e lo vedrò fra poco,
Quando, per bella amabile fortuna,
Contento, e lieto di me stesso i giorni
Passar vedrammi ognun che al fuso eterno
L' immite Parca tutto dì mi fila
E tutt' altra sarò da quel che or sono.

It may not be amiss to add a translation on the next page
for the benefit of those who cannot follow the original;
which, it must be owned, is rather verbose, and yet cramped
in expression. It shall be as literal as possible.

VERSES BY THE MARQUIS HERCULES CONSALVI
AMONG THE ARCADIANS, FLORIDANTE ERMINIANO
ON RETURNING TO RESUME HIS STUDIES

ME,—who recall my willing steps, to tread
Once more the course of studious toil, relieved
By noble arts; who lure from dreamy flights
The thoughts and fancies which, with rapid strokes,
Imagination artist-like creates;—
Me smiling greet, and tenderly embrace,
Pallas! the friend and only soothing stay,
Or rather certain joy of him, whose lips
The Nine who dwell on the Parnassian hill
Were first to moisten with their purest milk.

"Put by thine aegis, lay aside the spear
That arms thy hand with terror, and affrights
The timid heart that dwells in gentle breast.
Tritonian Goddess!—Daughter of great Jove!—
Bestow thine aid; the path whereon I tread
Make smooth and straight; my yearning burn on high.
With thee propitious I will haste along,
And cheerful wipe my moist and pallid brow.
If, when on either side I look for thee,
I see thee, Goddess! more than is thy wont,
Regard me kindly, with a gracious eye,
And on thy rosy lips a cheerful smile;
That smile alone, yet more a soothing word,
Will still my panting heart, and give me breath.

"Then come, indeed, with gruff and sidelong gaze,
From the rough caverns, 'neath her beetling brows,
And with her hollow cheeks and sallow skin,
Hard-fisted and hard-minded, cheerless Toil;
And threaten me with long and weary watch,
By night, and straining breathless work by day.
For, by thee guided, I will make but light
Of cramping labour, and of anguish dire.
That Dame unjust, with strength and patience armed
I will defy; with adamantine breast
Will bend her head, and yoke her to my car.

"Yes, I will reach the goal, which sweet Desire,

Most noble offspring, as she boast, of Hope,
Points to, with flattering look that wins my heart,
There—oh, I know it!—honour, glory, wealth,
Await me, goad and prize to honest deeds.
Certain is this my lot: this is the web
Woven for me in heaven's unfailing loom.
  "But stay—dream I, perchance? or does some God
Benignant whisper to me happy truths?
No, no, I dream not; full soon shall I know it,
When all shall see me, by fair Fortune's love,
Pass through the days which Fate unsparing spins
On her eternal distaff for my destiny,
Joyful, contented with myself; for then
Far other shall I be than now I am."

Success waited on this precocious confidence, and to
what extent the patronage which he early won assisted the
youthful poet, cannot be fully known. Probably, however,
York[1] did him better service than Pallas. Consalvi passed
through the usual preliminary steps, by which the cardinalate is attained, *in curia*; for he never was a nuncio
abroad; nor did he ever take priest's orders, so as to be
more immediately employed in purely ecclesiastical administration. On the 11th of August, 1800, he was named
Cardinal Deacon of the Church of St Mary ad Martyres,
better known as the Pantheon.

Although he early enjoyed the confidence of Pius VII, it

1. There are several medals of the Cardinal Duke, commemorating his title.
One is rather a coin struck in his name, *sede vacante*,—this being the privilege of the Vice-chancellor at such periods. It bears the royal arms of
England, Scotland and Ireland, surmounted by a cardinal's hat over a ducal
coronet. On the reverse is the legend, "*Henricus Cardinalis Dux Ebor S.R.E.
Vice-cancellarius. Sede vacan. 1769.*" Another is a large medal with his portrait, and nearly the same inscription, with the addition of *Ep. Tuscul.* On
the reverse is a figure of Religion, with his crown and hat at her feet, and the
legend round, "*Non desideriis hominum, sed voluntate Dei.*" [Not by men's
desires but by the will of God.] On the exergue is the date 1766.

was not until a later period that his extraordinary powers became known and admired throughout Europe. So distingushed, indeed, was he among the Roman *prelatura*, that the Sacred College assembled in the conclave which elected Pius VII at Venice, in 1800, chose him for their secretary, and he was immediately named pro-secretary of State by the new Pontiff.

At the period of Pius's removal from Rome and Italy, Cardinal Consalvi did not hold the highest office, which, as we have seen, was occupied most worthily by Cardinal Pacca. But he shared his sovereign's exile, and was one of the "black cardinals" of Paris, that is, one forbidden to wear the distinctive colour of his order. After this period began that prosperity of public life, which shone so brightly in his youthful vision. For one, who had been educated in the comparative seclusion of the Roman government and court, to find himself suddenly transferred from this, and even from banishment, into contact with the most brilliant array of camp and court celebrities which Europe had ever seen united, and, what is more, with the council of such statesmen, most cunning in their craft, as sovereigns could bring together to watch over their interests, and to have to play his part among them, with skill, with tact, and with success equal to any, was a position and a task to which only genius of a high order could be equal. And this, certainly, Consalvi was found to possess. The Emperors of Russia and Austria, the Kings of Prussia and France, Wellington and Blücher, Metternich, Castlereagh, and a host of plenipotentiaries of claimants of states and principalities, and representatives of every form of government, had to be made acquaintance with, to be gained, and to be treated with, by the representative of one, whom all no doubt respected, but to whom all were not so ready to be generous, if even just. In the settlement of claims, and the adjustment of pretensions which were about to ensue, Conslavi was deputed by the Pope to regain for him and his successors the many provinces of which he had been stripped. This was a difficult and a delicate task. But before pressing forward to the conclusion of this matter, we must dwell on an interesting episode in it.

In the June of 1814, the Emperor of Russia and the King of Prussia visited London; and many will remember the fêtes, splendid but somewhat childish, which greeted them. The writer retains them among his holiday reminiscences,[1] for they took place in vacation time: and they belonged decidedly to the age of pavillions and pagodas. At the same time Cardinal Consalvi crossed the Straits, and appeared in London. He was bearer of a brief, or letter, to the Prince Regent, from the Pope. Let it be remembered, that the penal laws were as yet in force, and that the dreadful penalty of *praemunire* cut off all friendly commerce between the ruler of these realms and the Head of the Catholic Church. How this first Cardinal who had landed in England since the days of Pole[2] was treated and received, will best be learnt from the account which Pius VII gave of the event, in his Allocution to the Consistory of September the 4th, 1815.

"The Cardinal, having quickly reached Paris, and having discharged these duties which we had confided to him towards his most Christian Majesty;[3] and having been received with that interest and affection to us which it was natural for us to expect from his piety and religion, proceeded to London without delay; whither the other sovereigns, with the exception of our beloved Son in Christ, Francis Emperor of Austria, had gone. And here we cannot sufficiently express to you what feelings of joy and gratitude filled us, on learning what had occurred on that occasion, in that most splendid city, capital of so mighty a kingdom. For the first time for more than two hundred years, a Cardinal of the holy Roman Church, and moreover a Legate of this Apostolic See, appeared publicly in that

1. Wiseman was on holiday in London from school at Ushaw College.
2. Reginald Pole, Cardinal; Archbishop of Canterbury, 1556-8.
3. Napoleon I. The speech was made after the 1814 reconciliation.

city, by the kind and generous permission of the government, adorned with the distinctive badge of his dignity, in
the same way as if he had been in this our own city.

"And further, when he proceeded to an audience of His
Royal Highness, the Prince Regent of England, to present
our brief, and express the sentiments of admiration, friendship, and attachment which we entertain towards him, as
well as towards that valiant, and in so many ways illustrious, nation, he was received at the palace with such marks
of benevolence and of kindness for us whom he represented, as could with difficulty have been exceeded. On which
account, professing ourselves deeply obliged to that prince,
and to the different orders that compose that generous
nation, towards which we always entertained great good-
will, we most gladly seize such an occasion to attest thus
publicly our esteem, and our lively gratitude."

The Pope goes on to say that in this city the Cardinal set
vigorously about his work, laying before the monarchs here
assembled the claims of the Holy See to the restoration of
all its dismembered provinces. The success of this first
appeal made the Pope rejoice, as he himself tells us, at the
selection which he had made of his minister.

It was, however, at the Congess of Vienna that the diplomatic battle had to be fought. The decree of Napoleon of the
10th of February, 1814, which released the Pope from captivity, restored to him only the Departments of Rome and of
Thrasymene. The richest and fairest of his provinces were
still to be regained: and they were tempting additions to
more powerful dominions. The ability, perseverance, and
admirable tact of Cardinal Consalvi won them back. He
seems to have been quite in his place among the most acute
diplomatists of the assembly. He even gained their admiration and esteem; and of none more than of the representative
of England. It is said that Lord Castlereagh[1] remarked of him
that he was the master of them all in diplomatic skill.

1. In his will Consalvi left small legacies to Lord Castlereagh's family.

His efforts were crowned with complete success, as to the great objects of his mission. He had right, indeed, on his side; but in great political congresses, the interests of the weak are often sacrificed to the wishes of the strong, under the guise of general principles, or of simpler balances, which require the rounding of large sums by the absorption of fractions. He always used to say that he received generous support from the representatives of Great Britain and Prussia; and on one point—the precedence of nuncios among ambassadors—the Pope, in the allocation above quoted, makes particular mention of this assistance. All obstacles were at length overcome; about the middle of June 1815, Monsignor Mazio, Secretary to the Cardinal Plenipotentiary, arrived in Rome from Vienna, with the welcome tidings, that the three Legations, the Marches of Ancona, and the Duchies of Benevento and Ponte Corvo, had been recognised as integral parts of the Papal States. The Cardinal energetically protested against the retension of the French possessions, and of the territory beyond the Po.

If the reader wishes to know the character of the statesman who, in his first essay, rose to the level of the old experienced ministers and negotiators of continental Europe, he shall have it in the words of an English lady, married into a noble French family, and remarkable for her shrewdness and keenness in determining character. She had the honour of receiving Cardinal Consalvi into her house at Rouen, during his exile in France: "Perhaps," said she, a few years after, to an intimate friend of the Cardinal's, "you will be surprised to hear what I am going to tell you, as to the opinion which I formed of your tutor at Vienna, before he had been a fortnight in my house. *True* humility in a most extraordinary and heroic degree is the characteristic of this Cardinal, and therefore he must have been the first politician at the Congress of Vienna."

When he returned to Rome, he had to undertake the reorganisation of the entire state after years of dismemberment, the formation of a new magistracy, and the reestablishment of new municipal, financial, and ecclesiastical systems. Of the manner in which much of this was done this is not the place to treat. It will be sufficient to observe that, through the remainder of the pontificate, the entire rule might be said to rest upon his shoulders; that, while the Pope gave him his full confidence, and trusted him as Pharaoh trusted Joseph, he was indefatigable, single-hearted, devoted, mind and soul, to the service of his master. He seemed to care for no other object. He had, of course, his opponents in policy, perhaps rivals of influence. A man placed, not so much in an elevated, as in a singular position, must disturb many below him,—

> *Urit enim splendore suo qui praegravat artes*
> *Infra se positas.*"[1]

But he seems to have borne all opposition, and even obloquy, with equanimity and placid forbearance.

His habits were most simple. There was no luxury about him in house or person. His dress was not more than decent. His tastes were refined. If in early youth he attracted the notice of an eminent patron by his taste and skill in music, he became in his turn the friend and protector of another, to whom music was a profession. This was Cimarosa, the well-known composer of *Matrimonia segreto*, and of much excellent sacred music. Like Mozart, he composed a splendid Requiem, which he dedicated to his friend the Cardinal. He, in his turn, had it executed for the first time at the composer's obsequies performed by his orders.[2]

Connected with his diplomatic missions, is an anecdote relating to a man of singular acquirements. While at Vienna, many learned men from all parts of Germany were naturally introduced to him, and he was repeatedly asked how was

1. Horace: Epistle 2.1.13. [For he glows with his own brightness which puts into shadow lower order skills.]
2. Domenico Cimarosa was born in Naples in 1749, and died in Venice in 1801.

Ignatius De Rossi. The Cardinal felt mortified at not being
able to answer, for, to tell the truth, he did not know whom
they meant. One of his first cares, on returning to Rome, was
to search after him; and certainly the inquiry, in some respects,
cannot have been satisfactory. He would find an old man, as I
have often seen him, dressed in an old cassock, and a coeval
cloak, tottering, as he leaned on his stick and muttered to himself, up and down the immeasurable corridors of the Roman
College, or sat in one of the recesses that gave them light. Day
after day have I and others seen him, and respectfully saluted
that wreck of a rare genius, and of learning scarcely surpassed;
and a courteous gleam lighted up his lack-lustre eye, as he
unfailingly returned the greeting. He was indeed past caring
for anything, though he wanted for no comfort. During these
last years of mental helplessness, through which he would
brook no control, his room, left always unguarded, had been
pilfered of rich treasures of learning; among them of the manuscript of a huge Arabic lexicon, which he would never publish,
from his horror of correcting proofs.[1] He used to say, after the
printing of his other works, that if the tempter had to deal
with another Job, and wished to make him lose his patience,
he would induce him to try his hand at publishing an Oriental

1. This extraordinary man is not so generally known as his illustrious name-
sake and contemporary at Parma, the collector of the greatest number of
Hebrew manuscripts ever brought together. Yet in learning, extensive and
deep, he was much his superior. In 1788, he published at Rome his *Commen-
tationes Laertianae*. Some one has said, "If you wish to appear learned, quote
Diogenes Laertius." But this is really a work of deep reading and rare acquaintance with ancient philology and philosophy. After a long interval, in 1807,
he published, at the Propaganda press, his *Etymologia Aegyptiana*. It was a
valuable precursor to Young and Champollion's discoveries; for it treats, in
alphabetical order, of all the Egyptian words quoted in ancient writers,
sacred and profane, with an immense spontaneous flow of varied erudition,
Rabbinical, Oriental, classical, and patristic. On the receipt of this wonderful
work, the Academy of Leipzig held an extraordinary meeting, and wrote a
most complimentary letter to the author. This was mentioned to Cardinal
Consalvi at Vienna. The Cardinal had been absent from Rome for some
years. The memory of this learned and most modest man can only be com-

work. However, the Cardinal added to his comforts, by immediately granting him an additional pension.

The Cardinal's affections were warm and faithful. Those
who were officially connected with him were sincerely
attached to him; and those whom he received to audience,
after they had gained his esteem, would be welcomed with a
cordial embrace. The chief sharer, however, of his dearest
affection was his brother, the Marquis Andrew Consalvi.
He was ten years younger, but he predeceased the Cardinal
by eleven years, dying in 1813. The latter, however, never
forgot their tender love, and kept a compact made between
them of sharing but one grave. Accordingly, in the Pantheon, where, as its Deacon, he ought to have been buried,
only a cenotaph, or rather an urn containing his heart, pre-
serves his memory; with an inscription and bust erected by
subscription of his many friends. But in the Church of St.
Marcellus is a modest tomb, on which it is inscribed that
there repose the bodies of the two brothers:—

QVI . CVM . SINGVLARI . AMORE . DVM . VIVEBANT
SE . MVTVO . DILEXISSENT
CORPORA . ETIAM . SVA
VNA . EADEMQVE . VRNA . CONDI . VOLVERE.[2]

pared to that of Magliabecchi, and other such prodigies. I will give one example of it, related to me by a witness, his fellow-professor, the late Canon
Lattanzi. When once at *villeggiatura*, at Tivoli, De Rossi offered, on being
given a line in any of the four great Italian poets, to continue on, reciting a
hundred lines, without a mistake. No one thought it possible; but, to the
amazement of all, he perfectly succeeded. He was then asked, if he would do
the same with the Latin classics, to which he replied: "It is twenty years since
I read the Italian poets, and then it was only for amusement: of the Latin
classics I have been professor, so you had better not try me." The late Cardinal Cappaccini, secretary and friend to Cardinal Consalvi, used to tell how,
when he was one of De Rossi's pupils in Hebrew, if the scholars wished to
shirk the lesson, they would put a question to their professor, who would start
off on a lecture in reply that might have been taken down and published: a
marvellous tessellation of Greek, Latin, Hebrew, and Italian quotations.
2. [Who with a rare love took delight in each other while they lived, and
wished that their bodies should be buried in the same tomb.]

In the transaction of business, the Cardinal Secretary of State was most assiduous. In addition to the burthen of his manifold duties, he had, according to Italian custom, to devote certain hours of the day to audiences, not bespoken beforehand, but granted to all ranks and all descriptions of persons. His memory and accuracy in the discharge of his often irksome duty were wonderful. After he had admitted separately all those whose position or known business entitled them to this distinction, he sallied forth into his ante-room, filled with humbler suppliants. He passed from one to another, heard with patience what each had to say, took his memorial from his hand, and named a day for his answer. Female petitioners were admitted separately, often while he partook of his solitary and simple meal in the middle of the day when they were allowed more scope for prolixity of speech. To those who came for their replies, he was ever ready to give them, in writing or by word of mouth; and it is said, that seldom or never[1] did he mistake a person, or his business, though he had only learnt them for the first time some weeks before.

1. I remember an exception which was quoted. A little stout man, with an irresistibly comic countenance, whom I recollect as a dilettante singer of buffo songs at private parties, and whose name was Felci, had applied for a situation. When his name was announced, the Cardinal mistook it for that of an *employé*, with a name very similar, as Delci, who had been guilty of some neglect of duty, and who had been summoned to receive a scolding. This fell on the head of the innocent aspirant, and at first overwhelmed him with its pelting storm of reproaches. He gradually began to see through the tempest, and to recover his breath. He perceived the mistake, waited until the hail-cloud had passed, threw himself, or rather subsided, into his own naturally good-humoured looks, and replied to the Cardinal, —"Your Eminence is mistaken;—

> *Quello è magro, ed io grasso;*
> *Quell è alto, ed io basso;*
> *Quell è impiegato, ed io sto a spasso.*"

Wiseman translates: "That man is lean, and I am stout; /He is a tree, and I'm a sprout;/ He is *in* place, and I am *out*."

It need hardly be added, that this improvisation dispelled all anger, and procured the petitioner what he had come to sollicit.

The poem which we have quoted, as the youthful vaticination of his future greatness, mentioned "wealth" as one of those blessings towards which his eager mind seemed to bound forward. That he accumulated, through the income of his offices and benefices, a considerable fortune, there is no doubt. But he lived without luxury, and in the papal palace free of many charges, and with the utmost simplicity; he certainly spent very little on himself, and he was no lover of money. Whatever he had saved, he left chiefly for religious and charitable purposes. By his will, he bequeathed his diplomatic presents, three very rich snuff-boxes, to complete the unfinished fronts of three churches, Araceli, the Consolazione, and San Rocco. He left trifling legacies to friends, among others to the Duchess of Devonshire, and some of Lord Castlereagh's family, and to the Duchess of Albany, a graceful acknowledgment of his obligations to the Stuarts, of whom she was the last representative. The bulk of his property he willed to Propaganda for the support of foreign missions, subject to annuities to his dependents, one or two of which remain unexpired.

The Pope and his minister seemed providentially made for each other. The comprehensive and energetic mind of Consalvi, his noble views and industrious love of details, filled up that void which might otherwise have succeeded the restoration, and have created disappointment, after the admiration and love that years of exile had won for the Pontiff. The wise and gentle and unshaken confidence of the prince gave ample room for expansion to the abilities and growing experience of the minister. Without the one the other would have been useless; and whichever failed first seemed sure to lead to the extinction of the other. Indeed they fitted so truly together, that even physically they may be said to have proved equal. The amount of vigour, health, and power meted out to the secretary was in just proportion to his need of them. He retained them as long as they were required by him for whose comfort and glory they had been intrusted to him.

The Pope died on the 20th of August, 1823, and his successor, Leo XII, was elected on the 28th of September
following. Of course there were different sentiments preva-
lent in Rome concerning Consalvi's principles of
administration. Every prime minister falls, more than most
men, under the Horatian principle,

> ...*Laudatur ab his, culpatur ab illis.*[1]

The new Pope belonged perhaps to another school of politics, or he may have entertained less friendly feelings
towards the person of Consalvi. At any rate Cardinal della
Somaglia, a man of high merit and character, was named
Secretary of State. But it is doubtful whether the broken
health of Consalvi would have allowed him to continue in
office. Probably he had outlaboured his strength, and had
concealed the failings of his health under exhausting
efforts, so long as his good patron required his assistance. In
the journal kept by a warm admirer of the Cardinal, I find
the following entry as early as Nov. 4: "—Saw Card. Consalvi. He is unwell. He rejoices at the success of the
students at the Concorso (competitive examinations).
Inquired how the news of the Pope's death had been
received in England," whence the writer had just returned.
"I told him he was universally praised and lamented, even
in the London papers." By December he had been obliged
to seek rest and a mild climate at the modest little sea-town
of Porto d'Anzo, but derived no benefit from the change.
The journal above quoted says: "Tuesday, 13 Jan. 1824. Saw
Card. Consalvi, who was in bed, fallen away and pale, very
little better from his residence at Anzo." Yet now, indeed,
his lamp rallied for a short time; sufficient to give proof of
its brilliant light, just before expiring. The Pope, himself
confined to his bed, and so ill that on Christmas eve he was
not expected to live to the morrow, had sent for the Cardinal, who went from his bed to see him. From that moment,
all difference was at an end. Two generous minds, hitherto

---

1. Horace: Satires 1.2.11. [*He is praised by some and blamed by others.*]

estranged, met, and recognised each other's worth. There was instantaneous forgetfulness of the past: and a silent understanding for the future. To the astonishment of many, the Pope named Consalvi Prefect of Propaganda, a most honourable and influential post. This was on the 14th of January. The next day he was for hours closeted with his sovereign, and in the frankest and clearest manner laid before him his whole scheme of politics, home and foreign. "Live," he said to him among many things, "and Catholic Emancipation will take place in England, under your pontificate. I have worked hard for it, having begun when in London."

Leo XII, expressing his admiration of the man and of his measures, seemed filled with new hopes, and inspired with fresh courage. He consulted him frequently; and it was confidently expected that he would soon restore him to his former post. But the faithful minister had run his course, had fulfilled his mission at the death of Pius. On the 22nd, confined to his bed, he signed letters demissory for several students at the English college: on the 24th important papers were sent to him from the pope. He desired the messenger to tell the Holy Father, who had asked if he could do anything for him, that the only thing he could do was, to send him the last apostolic blessing, received by cardinals on their death-bed. It was brought by Cardinal Castiglione, his greatest friend; and at half-past one he calmly went to rejoin, in a better world, the master whom he had faithfully served, and the friend whom he had affectionately loved.

… "Quos ignea virtus
Innocuos vitae, patientes aetheris imi
Fecit, et aeternos animam collegit in orbes."[1]

1. [Those whom fiery virtue kept innocent in life and forbearing of its base atmosphere, and gathered in soul into the heavenly realms.]
  Two days after his death, the Pope said to Mgr. Testa, "'Che cosa mi ha detto quell' uomo, l'ultima volta che l' ho veduto!' Then hanging down his head, he added: 'Ma sembra che Dio vuol castigarmi in tutte le maniere.' "
—M.S. Journal.

CHAPTER VII

POLICY OF PIUS THE SEVENTH'S GOVERNMENT

WITHOUT entering into any general considerations on the subject of government, or discussing its best forms, or even expressing any opinion about them; but, on the other hand, judging things in their own times and places, and by the only principles then and there applicable to them; one may say unhesitatingly that the government of Pius VII, through his Minister Consalvi, was just, liberal, and enlightened. No doubt, had that sovereign reenacted the laws under which his subjects had groaned as an oppression, and reestablished the republic which they still detested as a usurpation; had he acted in the teeth of all Europe, in spite of every principle which guided sovereigns and statesmen in his restoration; had he even thereby risked for himself another catastrophe, and for Italy another war, there might now-a-days be many who would extol him as a hero, almost deify him as a man beyond and above his age. Had he acted so, however, at that time, he would have been ridiculed, deserted, and abused by all parties, whig or tory, conservative or radical, as a fanatic, an unseasonable phenomenon, a man behind the age, which had outgrown revolutionary fancies; in fine, a dotard who had better have been translated from the cell of a prison to that of an asylum, than restored from exile to a throne. We doubt if even the sorry compliment of a newspaper paragraph would have been paid for his pains.

He was restored, as Pope, to the temporal government of the portion of Italy held by his predecessors, without share in the warlike achievements of other princes, without a claim to the prizes of their victories. He was restored concurrently by Protestant and Catholic powers, with the applause of the civilised world; and amidst the acclamations of joy, or rather in accordance with the longings, of his own subjects. He was restored on the principle which formed the basis of all restorations at the time;—that Europe, so long convulsed, and so long unsettled, should return to the normal state from which she had been wrenched. Empires were restored as empires, kingdoms resettled as kingdoms, grand-duchies as grand-duchies, republics as republics. And so the Pope was given back to Rome, to rule as Popes had done, by a system exceptional, and in a form the loss of which experience had proved to be hurtful. The independence of the Pope, that is, the combination in one of spiritual rule over the whole Catholic Church with temporal limited sovereignty, had been sensibly demonstrated to be an important element in the readjustment of Europe. The evils resulting from the subjection of the common Father of all the faithful to one of his more powerful children, had been universally felt; and the continuation of such an irregular condition by a peaceful subjugation of the ecclesiastical to any lay power, would have been only providing for the habitual derangement of religious action.

During the invasion of Northern Italy by the French in 1797, the Pope, then cardinal Bishop of Imola, had been placed in a situation of great difficulty, which required both tact and courage; and he had displayed both. While he retained the firmest fidelity to his sovereign, he exhorted his people to submit to the overwhelming power of the enemy, and not to tempt them, by an irritating and useless resistence, to put in execution their barbarous threats of universal massacre, and destruction by fire of cities and villages. A fierce and disorderly insurrection at Lugo proved how real and earnest was the menace. General Augereau, on the 8th of July, completely defeated the foolish patriots, and delivered their city to a sack, which in three hours stripped it of an incredible amount of plunder. It lasted no longer, because Chiaramonti, who had in vain addressed the inhabitants, humbled himself so far, as to cast himself on his knees before the French general, and refused to rise till the boon of mercy which he craved was granted.

His position, however, was too embarassing; and his friend, Pius VI called him to Rome. He entreated to be allowed to return to his people, to shield them from danger, when a new peril surprised him. The Austrians, subsidised by England, were for a short time masters of the province of Aemilia, and were approaching Imola, when the bishop considered it his duty to exhort his people to submit to them, as their liberators from the yoke imposed upon them. No sooner had the Austrians retired than he was accused of sedition. Instead of flying from the danger, he proceeded at once to the French head-quarters at Lugo, and there pleaded his own cause before the general, whom he knew to be most hostile to him, with such gentleness and firmness, as won from that soldier expressions of esteem and marks of honour.

His enemies, however, were not so easily satisfied; and the republican magistrates of Imola denounced him to the supreme authorities of Bologna, as having favoured the Austrians. Letters to him, from Cardinals Giannetti and Mattei, containing circulars addressed by them to their flocks in favour of Austria, were intercepted, and formed the ground-work of the charge; fabrications and exaggerations composed its superstructure. The French general, incensed, started at once with a large detachment of troops, proclaiming that the Cardinal should be severely punished, and his see rifled. The bishop[1] left his city by night, not to flee, but to face the danger. He was too good a shepherd to leave his sheep to the wolf, and escape their sacrifice. Boldly he directed his steps towards the approaching spoilers. The general was Macdonald. Chiaramonti met him face to

1. This was his third or fourth escape. At an earlier period, when the Cisalpine republic was established, he denounced it to his flock, and was accused to the Paris Directory, by the police of Milan. He vindicated himself so powerfully as not to be removed from his diocese. Again, he refused to take the "civic oath," as it was called, and was deprived of the maintenance (the *mensa*) of his see.

face: with apostolic freedom, he reproved him strongly for his intended barbarity, and vindicated frankly his own conduct. He prevailed and saved the city from destruction or devastation. It is not wonderful that his biographers should have compared this intrepid and generous conduct to that of St. Leo the Great meeting Attila.[1.]

When, only three years after these occurrences Chiaramonti found himself the occupant of the throne, the out-works of which he had so resolutely defended against republican and anti-Christian invasion, when he was placed at the head of a state, the outposts of which he had known so well how to guard, we cannot be surprised to see him only more determined in upholding the same principles of firm but prudent resistance, and consistent preservation of what he had received. The same courage in meeting an enemy face to face, and the same bold adhesion to duty, will be found blended with the same condescension, and readiness to avoid useless resistance and fruitless collision. Some things which at first sight might be considered as the result of weakness, may be traceable to this quality.

The first public acts of the new Pontiff showed that, nevertheless, he was above prejudices, and well understood sound principles of political economy. Besides excellent provisions for reforms in every department of public administration, in that of justice among others, two series of measures characterised the commencement of his reign. The first regarded free trade in provisions, and a considerable approach to it in other departments of commerce. There was a great and alarming scarcity of grain in Central Italy, the year of the Pope's accession, 1800. There was literally a *panic* in the public mind in consequence; and the exportation of cereals from the States was forbidden. But, by a decree issued in September of that year, free trade in

1. In 452 AD St Leo met Attila after his Hun tribesmen had sacked Milan, and the Pontiff persuaded him to accept tribute instead of pillaging Rome.

corn was permitted; and the corporation of bakers was abolished with its exclusive privileges, so as to make it free to all to bake and sell bread. All duty was taken off oil, and its free importation was permitted. These new measures took the public by surprise; but they were soon much extended. For, early in the following year, all provisions were brought under the same regulations; and five more sources of revenue were thrown open to public competition. The edict on this subject, the result of a special commission, was long, and entitled, "*Decree motu proprio on provisions and free trade;*" and bears the date of the 11th of March, 1801. The annual medal struck for the feast of SS. Peter and Paul that year bears the figure of Abundance, with a ship at its side, and the inscription:—

COMMERCIORUM PRIVILEGIA ABOLITA[1]

In the mean time the treasury was empty; the Treaty of Tolentino had drained every available resource; even the four tiaras, of immense price and beautiful workmanship,[2] had been stripped of their jewels to pay the ruinous contribution of six million dollars imposed on it in 1796. A new system of general taxation was necessary to supply the urgent and current wants of the government. This was published about the same period, prefaced by a candid but mournful acknowledgment of the exhausted condition of the public purse. The system involved a very complicated, but most important, operation, which was not fully carried out till 1803, that of embodying in the debts of the state those of provincial, or at least municipal governments, the state at the same time undertaking the administration of their real property, as security to itself.

As far as one can judge at this distance of time, it would appear that the internal policy, directed by Cardinal Consalvi

1. The privileges of traders are abolished.
2. One was from the golden period of Pope Julius II.

from the very outset, was enlightened, perhaps, beyond that of many greater states. That policy is the one pursued by the present Pontiff, who has been yearly reducing the duties, and other pressures upon import-commerce; and has been getting rid of monopolies, or rather, the farming of internal resources, with the most gratifying success.

Another evil of the past calamitous period had been the total depreciation of the coinage. A quantity of base metal, as well as copper currency, had been put into circulation, with artificial values, after 1793; and the usual ill-judged attempts had been resorted to, of raising them, when fallen in the market, by public authority. The last of these useless efforts, by the Commissioner Naselli, in 1800, before the Pope's arrival, had only produced embarassment and diminished commercial confidence. The Pope, however, and his minister took a better view of this monetary difficulty. Several schemes which had been proposed for clearing the country of debased circulation, whereby loss would have fallen heavily on the holders of it, were unhesitatingly rejected. Instead of this, a fair and current value was assigned to it, and it was received at the mint, and no more was reissued. This was in December, 1801, and on the 13th of January, 1802. In October the plan was completed. On the 5th of that month all the base coin was called in, and the government bore the entire loss. A million and a half dollars were paid out in silver, all over the States, and not a coin of inferior metal left in circulation. And from that day till the late republic, no country in Europe had a better or more abundant silver circulation than the Papal states.

The measure was, however, completed by the readjustment of all public contracts made under the previous condition of the money market; and tables were published giving the proportions between the values of the old and new coinages, so as to assist all classes to remodel existing engagements on an equitable basis.

Never was any measure more blessed, by the poor especially, than this. Hence, at the great event of the year, the medal for 1802 artistically perpetuates it with the legend:

MONETA . RESTITUTA.[1]

After the restoration, the cares of Government were even more heavy, but equally guided by a wise and generous spirit. Let it be remembered how late, and how astounding, was the great commercial revolution of free trade amongst us. The old corn-laws, the sliding scale, the mighty League, the extorted repeal of those laws, through the joint agency of the elements and of popular agitation, are so recent, that the refluent wave of the great movement is not yet still; but murmurs dully in quiet corners, where Conservative members feel themselves at home; amidst grumbling farmers; and occasionally breaks into a whisper in some eccentric parliamentary speech. But, even last year, great and enlightened states prohibited the exportation of corn and other sorts of food. In 1815, the Pope, while forbidding their exportation, not only permitted their free entry, but gave a premium on their introduction into the States, and a distinct one for their transmission into the provinces.

There were, however, more serious matters than these to occupy the thoughts of the sovereign and his ministry; and they were fully considered. Many religious houses and other establishments had been sold by the French government and had even been passed through several hands. On the 14th of August, 1816, all such properties as had not been materially altered, and which could thus again be restored to their original purposes, were demanded back; but the actual holders were all to be indemnified for their losses; and a commission *ad referendum* was appointed to examine individual claims, that they might be fully satisfied.

In order to distribute fairly the burthens of taxation, a new and complete survey and valuation of the entire property of cities and of the country were most accurately made,

1. Currency restored.

corresponding to the French Cadastre; perhaps in no country is it so exact as in Rome. A special commission soon accomplished this useful undertaking, while another prepared a new demarcation of provinces, or delegations, and governments, with their respective forms of administration and judicial arrangements. The result of the system so framed was that, notwithstanding the immense expenditure thrown on the state by the restoration, and the reparation of previous wrongs, a diminution of taxation to the extent of 200,000 dollars on the land tax was made in 1816. When we consider that the Government took on itself the obligations of the state before the occupation, and immense compensation for damages and losses; that in addition it laid out great sums in public works, and in promoting science and art; we may surely conclude that there must have been a wise administration to effect all this, without recurring to loans, or creating a foreign debt.

CHAPTER VIII

RELATIONS WITH ENGLAND

THERE is one remarkable feature in the external policy of Pius VII and Cardinal Consalvi, which deserves to be further noticed; the more so as to this the writer owes all his means of possessing recollections of late pontiffs. It has been already alluded to, and need not, therefore, detain us long.

Certainly, for three hundred years, with the exception of one very brief period, there never existed such friendly relations between the Holy See and the crown of Great Britain, as under the Seventh Pius. An admiration for this empire, and even an affection for it, seemed instinctive both in the Pope and in his minister. It is indeed well known, and scarcely needs repetition, that one of the avowed, perhaps principal causes of the rupture between

Pius and Napoleon was the refusal of the Pope to join actively in what was called the Continental system, that is, the exclusion of British goods, and all British commerce, from Continental ports and countries. This is a matter of history. But the personal calamities of the Holy Pontiff, his admirable patience and exemplary virtues, had, no doubt, their share in enhancing the sympathy due on account of the cause for which he suffered. More than once was England ready to receive him on board her ships of war, and give him asylum.

The journey of Consalvi to London has been mentioned, and with it the fact of his having conveyed letters from the Prince Regent to his Holiness. This mark of friendship was repeated when the Cavalier Canova, raised on the occasion to the title of Marquess of Ischia, returned to Rome, with the works of art restored from the Louvre. It is agreeable to relate, that the heavy expense of their removal from Paris to Rome was defrayed entirely by our government; and this act of generosity was enhanced by the letter from the Prince, of which Canova was bearer, as he was of letters from Lord Castlereagh to the Pope, and to the Secretary of State.

When Lord Exmouth had succeeded in his gallant attack on Algiers, he too wrote letters to both. That to the Holy Father was couched in terms as respectful as a Catholic could have used. It is dated Algiers, 31st of August, 1816, from on board the "Queen Charlotte." It informs the Pope of his success; declares that Christians' slavery is at an end for ever, and adds that he sends him 173 captives, subjects of his States. These, he hopes, will be a present acceptable to His Holiness, and will give him a title to the efficacy of his prayers.

It was a kind and grateful feeling towards England which led to the restoration of the national college that had existed so long in Rome. Cardinal Consalvi warmly took up its cause, assumed to himself the duties, though he would not accept the title, of "Cardinal Protector" to the establishment.

He assisted personally at the meetings of its superiors, and attended to all its details. A volume lies before me, a thick quarto manuscript, in almost every page of which there is a record of some kindness towards the Catholics of England. One instance only need be entered here.

The present church at Moorfields, which now serves as the pro-cathedral to the diocese of Westminster, was finished in 1820.[1] It was considered then as a spacious and handsome building. A perspective drawing of its interior was sent to Rome, and presented by the Rev. Dr. Gradwell to the Pope. The good Pius immediately said that he would send a token of his affectionate interest in the work. The papal treasury and sacristy were very empty; but he ordered the most valuable object in church plate that he possessed to be prepared for a present. His attendants remarked that it was the most costly thing he had; and his reply was, "There is nothing too good for me to give the English Catholics." On his restoration, the Chapter of Mexico had sent him a massive gold chalice, richly set with emeralds, pearls, and diamonds. It was accompanied by cruets, bell, and dish, all of the finest gold. This was his intended gift, and he commissioned Dr. Gradwell to have an inscription engraved upon it. On the 29th of April, he waited on His Holiness with two inscriptions. The Pope read them, and said that either would do, but that neither mentioned the consecration of the chalice by himself. He was answered that such an additional mark of kindness had not been presumed upon. The pontiff said it was his intention to give this further value to his gift; and it is

1. St Mary Moorfields in Eldon Street in the City of London is a newer church, built in the same style as the pro-cathedral using some of the materials of the old church—the fine columns are from the older building. The valuable site of the old pro-cathedral in Finsbury Circus in the City of London was sold to fund the new Metropolitan Cathedral of the Precious Blood in Westminster. Pius VII's chalice remained at St Mary Moorfields when the new cathedral was opened.

recorded in the inscription on the chalice, which is used at Moorfields on the greater solemnities.[1]

This chapter will not be unsuitably closed by the inscription which records, in the English College, the kindness of Pius and his minister in restoring that national establishment.

MEMORIAE

PII . VII . PONT . MAX .

QVOD . COLLEGIVM . ANGLORVM

A GREGORIO . XIII . P . M .

IN ANTIQVO EIVS NATIONIS ADVENARVM . HOSPITIO

PRIMITVS . CONSTITVTVM

VRBE . AVTEM . A . GALLIS . OCCVPATA

ANTE . AN . XX . DISSOLVTVM

ANNO . MDCCCXVIII . RESTITVERIT

EIDEMQVE . AD . VOTVM . NATIONIS . EIVSDEM

RECTOREM . DE . CLERO . IPSIVS . PRAEFECERIT

HERCVLE . CONSALVIO . S . E . R . CARD . COLLEGII . PATRONO

ANGLIAE . EPISCOPI . ET . CLERVS

GRATI . ANIMI . CAVSA.[2]

1. The inscription is as follows;— *"Pius VII. Pont. Max. Templo Londini in Moorfields, recens a Catholicis exstructo, a se consecratum libens donum misit. A.D.N. MDCCCXX. Pont. S. XXI."* [Pius VII, Pontifex Maximus, in the year of Our Lord 1820, and in the twenty-first year of his pontificate, expressly sends this gift, consecrated by himself, to the Church at Moorfields in London, which has recently been built by Catholics.]

2. "To the memory of Pius VII, Pontifex Maximus who, in 1818, restored the English College, which Gregory XIII, Pontifex Maximus, had first established as a hostel for English pilgrims in the ancient days of our nation, and which for 20 years had remained dissolved while the city was occupied by the French. In response to the prayer of the same nation he provided a rector for the College from the clergy, and His Eminence Cardinal Hercule Consalvi became its patron. The bishops and clergy have set this up in grateful thanks." In the MS journal before me, in the same page, is the following entry: "May 1. The King of England has written in Latin to the Pope with his sign manual (editor: whereby the royal signature is superscribed on the letter, then sealed with the privy signet or great seal to complete its validity). The first instance of such a correspondence since our revolution (1688). The Pope is pleased, and is answering it."

CHAPTER IX

LITERATURE, SCIENCE, ART

NEITHER of the foreign occupations, the republican or imperial, lasted sufficiently long to interrupt that succession of men devoted to study which Italy, and especially Rome, has always kept up. Indeed, after the restoration, there yet survived veterans who had gathered their first laurels on the fields of a peaceful country, unconscious for generatons of hostile invasion.

Such, for instance, was the antiquarian Fea, one of those men of the old school, like the Scaligers, the Vossii, or rather, Graevius and Gronovius, who could bring to the illustration of any subject a heap of erudition from every imaginable source, from classics or Fathers, from medals, vases, bas-reliefs, or unheeded fragments of antique objects, hidden amidst the rubbish of museum magazines. He is perhaps best known in the literary world by his magnificent edition of Winklemann, the notes to which are not inferior in value to the text. Indeed, one might say that the two authors divide the qualities of the book: the German bringing to it the taste and sagacity of the artistic antiquarian, and his Italian annotator the abundant, or even redundant, learning of the erudite but dry archaeologist.

Day after day might one see him, sitting for hours in the same place, in the library of the Minerva, at the librarian's desk, poring to the end of his life over old books still. And is it not always so? In youth we love new books, our own contemporaries, those that have our measure and that of the age, those who "catch the manners living as they rise." But as we grow old, we live backwards towards the past. We go willingly among those who in popularity are aged, or aging, like ourselves. They suited their era exactly, and were then liked by the young, and thrown aside, with a shake of the head, by the mature. But now that the superficial gloss is worn away, that which dazzled, and that which offended, how racy and how charming they become to us. Such are the memoirs, the letters, the journals, and the essays of former ages, their chronicles even, in their primeval quaintness. They may have represented, and no doubt did represent, fierce parties, gross enmities, sharp reproof, the envious eye, the venomed tooth, the wicked smile, the curled lip, or the lolling tongue. To us all the leer and jibe, and even playful malice, have softened down into harmless wit and gentle sprightliness.

Well, no matter, the *old* love to converse with the *dead*; and therefore it is not surprising that one should remember Fea with a parchment-bound book, folio or octavo, or perhaps a heap of many such before him. He was indeed an antiquarian of the old school, as has been remarked; and perhaps, had he been asked which method he preferred, the digging in the earth round ancient monuments, to discover their history and name, or the excavating them from old authors, and determining them by skilful combinations of otherwise unintelligible passages, he might have preferred the second method. His theories, based upon actual explorations, were certainly not happy, and his conjectures, though supported with ingenuity and erudition, were not verified by local searches. In this respect, Professor Nibby, partly his rival, though much his junior, was more successful.

The Abbate Fea was verily not a comely nor an elegant man, at least in his old age; he had rather the appearance of a piece of antiquity, not the less valuable because yet coated with the dust of years, or a medal, still rich in its own oxidization. He was sharp and rough, and decisive in tone, as well as dogmatic in judgment. If one went up to him, rather timidly, at his usual post, to request him to decipher a medal at which one had been poking for hours, he would scarcely deign to look at it, but would tell you at once whose it was; adding, perhaps for your consolation, that it was of no value.

A contrast to him in externals, was another priest, whose learning was as various, though of a totally different class; the Abbate Francesco Cancellieri. I remember him coming to pay his annual Christmas visit to the rector of the College, an octogenarian at least, tall, thin, but erect, and still elastic; clean and neat to faultlessness, with a courteous manner; and the smiling countenance that can be seen only in one who looks back serenely on many years well spent. He used to say, that he began writing at eighteen, and had continued till eighty; and certainly there never was a more miscellaneous author. The peculiar subjects of which he treats, and even the strange combinations in their very titles, are nothing, compared with the unlooked for matters that are jumbled and jostled together inside. Few would have thought of writing a volume on "the head physicians of the Popes;" or on "the practice of kissing the Pope's foot antecedently to the embroidery of the cross on his shoe;" or on "the three papal functions in the Vatican Church;" or on "men of great memory, or who have lost their memories;" or finally, "on the country houses of the Popes, and the bite of the tarantula spider." But the fact is this, that under these titles are to be found stray waifs and *trouvailles* of erudition, which no one would think of looking for there. Hence his works must be read through, to ascertain what they really contain. No clue to the materials of his books is given by the titles, or any other usual guide.

I remember a most promising young German scholar, cut off before he had time to fulfil the expectations of his friends. This was Dr. Pappencordt, whose *History of the Vandals* had early gained a literary prize in his own country. His acquaintaince with mediaeval history was amazing; he remembered the dates of the most insignificant events; and would make excursions into the desolate border tracts in the mountains, between Rome and Naples, to visit the theatre of the most puny action between pugnacious barons in Central Italy. I dwell with pleasure on his memory; for many an interesting bit of information, which has not been without its use, did I collect from him, on topics of Italian history, whereof one did not find clever men take much heed. He was still, as I have intimated, very young: and he had all the amiable and candid worth which belongs to the youthful enthusiast. But already, as he informed me, he had gone through the whole of Baronius's Annals, extracting from them a list of every historical document referred to in that immense and unrivalled compilation; but he had experienced the misfortune, to which every accumulator of inky sheets is liable, of seeing just the last of them taken at the end of winter to light the stove, by that deadliest enemy of literary litter, the tidy housemaid.

Well, this industrious young scholar told me, that he had for years been searching for a document which he knew must exist somewhere, but which he had nowhere been able to find. It was this. The Council of Trent was transferred after the seventh session to Bologna, where the eighth and ninth sessions (merely formal ones) were celebrated. The ground alleged was the existence of contagious or epidemical disease in Trent, which made it dangerous to the life of the prelates to meet there. This is distinctly stated in the decree of the eighth session, of the 11th of March, 1547. Of course, the adversaries of the Council gave another reason, and denied the reality of the one alleged. The German historian was desirous of finding the medical certificate or declaration alluded to in the Decree, and mentioned but never given by historians. At length, while plunging through a tangled jungle, the produce of Cancellieri's unchecked fertility, his work on the Papal *villeggiaturas* and the tarantula, he lit most opportunely on the very document, like a solitary flower in the wilderness. It was there given textually from the original.

It was thus that he may be said to have verified the character which Niebur, one of the learned foreigners in Rome at the time of these recollections, gave to Cancellieri's writings; that "they contained some things that were important, many things that were useful, and everything that is superfluous."

One of the most useful features of his writing is, that on whatever subject he treats he gives you the fullest list of authors upon it compiled till his time. Thus, his work on memory contains a catalogue of writers on artificial memory, and of inventors of various systems of it, which would probably surprise most readers.[1]

Miserable as were the times that had just preceded our epoch, for all who had made the Church or her studies their choice, many were then engaged in the cultivation of sacred literature who have since distinguished themselves in it. But the men of the period belonged to the training of a former age. It could not interest the ordinary readers of these pages to enumerate them, especially as few at that time had spirits, or occasion, to become authors in a science which was but little encouraged. Complete silence, however, might be interpreted as an admission that Rome was defective in what had always formed its special pursuit; and therefore we will be content with saying, that there were many men whose cultivation of sacred studies prepared the way for the solid ecclesiastical learning which now flourishes in Rome.

One man celebrated throughout Europe, whose researches embraced every branch of learning sacred and profane, may be expected to find a brief notice here, did not the object of the work naturally assign him to another place. Although Angelo Mai made his first appearance in Rome

1. Such an author may well be supposed to have got together, in the course of his long life, a most miscellaneous and extensive collection of tracts, pamphlets, and papers. This came into the hands of the Marchese Marini, editor of "Vitruvius" and "De Marchi," both on a magnificent scale; who also became possessor of the collection of Miscellanea formed by the celebrated antiquarian Enea Quirino Visconti, who preferred Paris to his native Rome. The two, with many additions, form a series of 300 volumes, or *cartons*, containing many things not easily to be found. They were included in the purchase of the magnificent Marini library, bought by the late Bishop Walsh, and given by him in perpetuity to the college of St. Mary's Oscott.

in 1819, and although the author well remembers the paragraph in the Roman paper which announced his arrival from Milan, and the subsequent one which proudly proclaimed his immortal discovery of Cicero's "*De Republica*," yet it was not till a later period that he could acquire, what he cherishes among his most valuable recollections, the kind and familiar intercourse enjoyed with this good and gifted man, not only in the shady alleys of the Pincian hill, but under other circumstances which brought them more closely together, and which were evidence of his kind and condescending disposition.

Before, however, leaving this portion of our desultory talk about literature, it may be permitted to say a few words upon a subject connected with it, and especially with its more sacred department. The pulpit is one of the best indexes of national taste in foreign literature. Indeed we can hardly except that of our own country. Terse and nervous language, conveying original thought and solid learning, is a proof of sterling literature having a hold on the national mind. When poetry in England, and inscriptions in Italy, were but a tissue of quaintnesses, forced conceits, sports with words, extravagant hyperboles, and turgid phraseology, the most admired orators of the day carried every such violation of good taste into the sanctuary; and no doubt they moved their sympathetic hearers to tears, as completely as they now do their occasional readers to laughter.

Schiller has scarcely caricatured F. Abraham a S. Clara in his "Piccolomini" for Germany; Fray Gerundio professes to give only real examples for Spain; and I think Dr. Beattie gives a few gems, from Dr. Pitcairn and other grave divines north of the Tweed, of absurd conceits. The classical Tiraboschi will supply examples of this debasement of the current literature of Italy, during the reign of what is there known under the chronological term of "*seicentismo*." A Latin inscription of the reign of Urban VIII could be dated, by reading three lines, as easily as by recognising the bees upon his shield. It is the same with the sonnets of the age. Language and thoughts fell together; the second pulled the first down to their own level; and they both dragged themselves along their dull and weedy path. Three Jesuit writers alone escaped this general corruption, Bartoli, Pallavicini, and Segneri. Traces may be discovered in them, especially in the latter, of the *concetti* so universal in the age; but still they form a trine exception to a characteristic mark of the time, as honourable to the body to which they belonged, on this account, as for the learning, piety, and ability which have made them standard authors in their various classes of ecclesiastical literature.

It would be easy to trace these analogies in bad taste still further into the arts. The "Barocco" in architecture, the "Berninesque" in sculpture, and "Mannerism" in painting, have clear relations, not only of time, but of character, with the literature to which we allude. It is quite possible that an improvement in either, or simultaneously in both, may take the form of a reaction, rather violent and intolerant at first. To a certain extent this has been the case in Italy. A foreigner perhaps has no right to judge; but there is no presumption in bearing witness to what only constitutes a fact analogous to what has been observed in every other language. The only way to purge any tongue of a bad taste which has eaten into it, or of a swarm of unidiomatic or foreign words that have made it almost a mongrel speech, is to return to a period antecedent to that of corruption, and to adopt a stern principle of excluding nearly every modern accession.

The Germans have been happy in their efforts to create a multitude of new words, which have superseded the modern bastard Gallo-German, and other interpolations of their noble tongue. They have used bodly the Horatian expedient of a "*callida junctura*" to create a fresh, but perfectly national, vocabulary. This required the cooperation of writers, popular as well as learned, who enjoyed the confidence, and the acknowledged leadership, of the whole German

PIUS THE SEVENTH 97

race. For such a literary combination we have neither the power nor will. But our own best writers, we feel, are those who have most naturally returned to tastes that preceded the vapid fluences and morbid elegances of the ante-Georgian period, rich though it be; and have sought to win back some of the nerve and sinew of the time, when choice could only lie between the greater or lesser preponderance of the classical or of the Saxon element.

In French it is essentially the same. One cannot read the modern poets, or even essayists, of the language, without observing the strong and successful effort to introduce what used to be denied to it—a distinct poetical language, employing words unused in the conversation or the writing of the drawing-room.

The Italian had a classical period to which he could return, a definite unalloyed standard of purity to which he might lead back his language. One writer reigned supreme there, and several others were near him, sufficiently varied in subjects and style to give breadth to the basis on which a regeneration could be grounded. Some indeed carried veneration, and consequent imitation, of Dante to extremes. But not only did such writers as Petrarch and Boccacio, poets or romancers, or the host of inferior novelists, impure in matter as pure in style, enter into the lists of models for the revival of good taste; but also most religious and ascetic writings, like the sweet "*Fioretti*" of St. Francis, the life and letters of St. Catherine, and the "Mirror of Penance" of Passavanti.

A return to the standard of literary excellence of that period was, therefore, perfectly compatible with a corresponding improvement in the most religious and spiritual class of writings. A danger of extravagance, or even of mistake, might indeed alarm; and examples are familiarly quoted of both, on the part of Father Cesari, the originator, in great measure, of the movement towards *purism*, as it was called. Objections of this sort are childish; no great change is effected without enthusiasm, and no enthusiasm can exist

without exaggeration, which of itself is a mistake. The
work has gone steadily on: and no one can compare the
Italian literature of the present day with that of the beginning of the century, and not perceive the immeasurable
gain. One Italian periodical alone, the *Civiltà cattolica* of
Rome, contrasted with any published formerly, will prove
the difference.

The influence of this change on the sacred eloquence of
Italy, has been just what might have been expected. In
some instances more essential requisites have been sacrificed to style; "the weightier things of the law" disappear
beneath the savoury seasoning of "aniseed and cummin;"
men's ears are tickled by a tissue of elegant paragraphs, and
by exquisite phraseology combined in harmonious periods.
It would be unjust to say that this was all that lately
attracted crowds to the preaching of the Avvocato Barberi,
who in mature age exchanged the forensic gown for the
cassock, and transferred his eloquence from the bar to the
pulpit. No doubt there were ideas as well as phrases in his
discourses; and ideas that proceeded from a vigorous and
cultivated mind. But men went to hear him as they went
to hear an elegant musician, who charmed, but changed
not, the listener; as one whose sermons of "judgment" ruf-
fled not the sinner, and put no sting into the wicked heart.
Graceful elegance was the substitute for stirring eloquence.

It is a common opinion that in Italy preaching is rather
of a character approaching to ranting, than akin to that
sober and guarded communication between clergyman and
parishioners which takes place once a week in a country
church. We shall not be far wrong if we place it, at various
points, between the two. Generally it has neither the
ignorant violence of the one, nor the tame common-place
of the other. Those who have been in Italy, and have frequented, with full comprehension of the language, the
sermons delivered every Sunday in the principal churches
of great cities, will acknowledge, whatever their religion
at home, that nowhere have they listened to discourses

containing more solid and useful matter, couched in more finished and yet simple language, or delivered in a more forcible yet unexaggerated manner.

To say that similar addresses would not be heard in the poorer quarters of towns, or in country villages, would be only to assert, that Italian priests have too much good sense, not to accommodate matter and manner to the characters and capacities of their audiences. Nevertheless it will be seen that day after day crowds of the poor will go to hear a preacher of eminence; for he would soon lose his high character, if he soared into regions whither the simple faithful could not follow him.

Foreigners, unfortunately, seldom trouble themselves about what does not come within the circle of fashionable ordinary occupation. Without, therefore, speaking of what would take an Englishman out of his reasonable distance from the region honoured by his residence, let any one attend the Sunday afternoon lecture on Scripture at the Gesù; and we will believe that he will hear as much plain practical instruction on Holy Writ, simply delivered, as he is likely to gather from sermons by popular preachers of ultra-biblical exclusiveness. Such certainly were the discourses continued for years by the late holy and learned F. Zecchinelli, a man deeply versed in the sacred writing; and delivered with that eloquence which manifests itself in look and speech, backed by life and conduct. No one could ever have reproached him with preaching up a scriptural rule of virtuous life, and not following it.

But besides the solid matter which one may often, indeed generally, hear in Italian sermons, there is a music accompanying it which gives it a winning charm, unknown to countries beyond the Alps. The grace of delivery seems to be one of the fine arts; for it lingers in their company, where they love to reside. The first Sunday after arriving in Rome, our party was taken to the church of the Araceli on the Capitol to hear a celebrated preacher deliver a sermon of his advent course. Hours before the time, the entire area

was in possession of a compact crowd, that reached from
the altar-rails to the door, and filled every aisle and all
available standing room. The preacher ascended the pulpit,
simply dressed in his Franciscan habit, which left the throat
bare, and by the ample folds of its sleeves added dignity to
the majestic action of his arms. His figure was full, but his
movements were easy and graceful. His countenance was
calm, mild, unfurrowed as yet by age, but still not youthful;
he seemed in the very prime of life, though he survived very
few years. To one who could not, except very imperfectly,
understand the language, and who had never heard a sermon in it, the observation of outward qualities and tokens
was natural, and likely to make an indelible impression.
Indeed, I remember no sermon as I do this, so far as the
"faithful eyes" go. And yet their ears had their treat too.
The first and merely unintelligible accents of that voice
were music of themselves. It was a ringing tenor, of metallic
brilliancy, so distinct and penetrating that every word could
be caught by the listener in every nook of the vast church,
yet flexible and varying, ranging from the keenest tone of
reproach to the tenderest wail of pathos. But the movement
and gesture that accompanied its accents were as accordant
with them as the graceful action of the minstrel, calling
forth a varied and thrilling music from the harp. Every look,
every motion of the head or body, every wave of the hand,
and the poise of the arm, was a commentary on the word
that it accompanied. And all was flowing, graceful and dignified. There was not a touch of acting about it, not an
appearance of attempt to be striking.

   Then, for the first time, I felt overawed by the stillness
which only the pent-up breath of a multitude can produce,
while some passage of unusual beauty and overpowering force
makes the hearer suspend, as far as he can, the usual functions
of life, that their energies may be concentrated on a single
organ. And scarcely less grand is the relief which breaks forth,
in a universal murmur, a single open breath from each one
swelling into a note that conveys more applause, or at least

approbation, than the clapping of twice as many hands.

Later, it was easier to feel, what the first day one could only wonder at. I remember, as the same preacher in the choir of St. Peter's uttered one of those sublime passages, feeling as if I lay prostrate in spirit, before a passing vision, scarcely daring to move or even turn the eyes aside. He was reproving negligence in attending at the celebration of the divine mysteries; and imagined the priest, rapt into heaven, and ordered to offer the heavenly sacrifice on the altar of the Lamb there. He painted with glowing words the attitudes, the countenances, and the feelings of adoring spirits, while for once only assisting at what is, in the Church militant, a daily privilege.

Now, if any one will turn to the *printed* sermons of Father Pacifico Deani, he may find the very sermons alluded to, and wonder that they can have been thus described. While far from pretending to make comparisons between the peerless master-piece of ancient eloquence and the humble Franciscan's devout discourses, one may be allowed to answer the objection by which Aeschines enhanced his great and successful rival's merit: "What if you had heard him speak them?" This, no doubt, was great part of the charm,—greater to one who, till then, had been accustomed only to the stately monotony in which the simplest lessons are often conveyed, and the unimpassioned tameness with which the most touching scenes are described, or rather narrated, at home.[1]

At the period on which we are engaged, science was efficiently represented in Rome. Professors Conti and Calandrelli are well known in the annals of astronomy for

1. F. Pacifico, a peasant child, was heard by a religous, preaching to a group of poor children of his own age. It was found that, after hearing a sermon once, he was able to repeat it almost word for word. He was educated, and became one of the most eloquent preachers of his time. He used to dictate a sermon to a secretary, and then preach it without reading it over. This he only required if, after a lapse of years, he wished to repeat the discourse.

the regularity and accuracy of their observations, annually published, in the Roman observatory, and by other valuable contributions to mathematical science in its highest branches. They were inseparable companions and most faithful friends. The first was still the professor whose lectures we attended; the second, a good old man, had retired from public duties. Pius VII encouraged first, then chartered and endowed, an academy or society, yet existing, for practical science, established by Profesor Scarpellini, and having its seat in the Capitol. Dr. Morichini, besides being a most able physician, was the friend and often co-labourer of Sir Humphry Davy, who made many experiments at the Sapienza in Rome, to which he was warmly attached. Dr. Morichini was the first who discovered, and applied, the magnetising power of the violet ray in the prism.

It would be easy to add a list of names of persons well versed in science who then lived and wrote, as Settele, Richebach, Vagnuzzi, and the numerous professors at the University; but names like those of the late F. Vico, and the living F. Secchi, are still better known to scientific Europe, in proof that Rome is not behind other great cities in its scientific attainments.

The reign of Pius VII was, in spite of its vicissitudes, most propitious for art. What has been said about language, may, in some measure be extended to this. The condition to which it had sunk could be remedied only by a complete transfer of affection and principle, from this to a better, indeed a faultless, period. And what could that be but the period of classical art, alone supreme in sculpture? There was in fact no other school. The early Christian, that of the Pisans, was itself a noble effort to revive the beauty of the heathen school, chastened by the feelings of a better religion; the strong development by Michelangelo was the burst of individual genius, not to be imitated by any less than himself. The intermediate period presented neither models sufficient, nor principles distinct enough, to become the basis of a new system of glyptic art. To Canova undoubtedly belongs the praise of having revived, or raised from a low state of affectation, exaggeration, and meanness of conception, this simplest of artistic resources for exciting grand ideas of God's noblest earthly creation, in the minds of the beings on whom he conferred that dignity. Canova's monument to Clement XIV took the world of art by surprise; and his return to the simple beauty, the calm attitudes, the quiet folds, the breadth and majesty of ancient works, soon put him at the head of the European school. And if he has been surpassed in some things by his followers, for example, by the great Dane, Thorwaldsen, it must never be forgotten that no step in excellence, not even the last to perfection, is equal to the stride from grovelling degradation to healthy action and truthful principle; especially when this at once places him who makes it in a preeminence that becomes a standard for rival excellence. And such certainly was Canova's position.

But the same principles will not hold good in painting. Besides our having very little to show us how the ancients practised this branch of art, we have another period of our own, which imparts to us all the practical instruction we could possibly require. Instead of this a cold classical school sprung up in Europe, of which David was the type in France, and the Cammuccinis in Italy; which sought its subjects in an unclean mythology or a pagan heroism, and its forms in the movementless and rigidly accurate marbles of antique production. A raw unmellow colouring, overbright and unblending, devoid of delicacy and tenderness, clothed the faultless design of the figures; so that the cartoon was often more agreeable than the finished painting. There, however, you saw riders, guiding their foaming steeds without a bridle, soldiers dealing heavy blows at one another with invisible swords, of which they grasped tightly the bladeless pommel. And this was, because the ancients so scupltured cavaliers and combattants, from the difficulty of providing them with a floating rein or a brandished sabre in so frail a material as marble. Why should not the eye have been as well left without an iris? There is, indeed, in the Hospital of Santo Spirito, in Rome, a ward painted in fresco, with countless figures, all somehow made eyeless; but this was the caprice, or malice, not the classicism of the artist.

This last yet reigns too much in Italy, where has sprung up, in the mean time, that beautiful German school, which at Munich, Cologne, Düsseldorf, and Berlin, has produced such lovely works; and which, still faithful to the land that gave it birth, is there nobly blooming with sweet grace, but is gradually shedding its seed on the fertile ground around it; repaying in Christian beauty the classical accuracy which fed its own root.

It must be acknowledged that such works in painting as were executed during the pontificate of Pius VII in the library, or museum, to commemorate its great events, are little worthy of their subject, or of Italian art.

The mention of these seats of learning and art suggests a few words. It is almost a matter of course, that every Pope adds to the treasures of the Vatican, both literary and artistic. In the earlier portion of his pontificate, Pius had already walked in his illustrious predecessors' footsteps. The Museo Pio-Clementino, the additon of his two immediate predecessors, seemed to leave him little hopes of surpassing it. The magnificence of its halls, the variety of its collections, and the beauty of many among its sculptures, combined the splendour of a palace with the richness of a gallery. The earlier contributions of our Pope were simple but most valuable. The long corridors leading to the Vatican library were filled by him with secondary monuments, urns, cippi, sarcophagi, altars, busts and statues, some of great price; and the walls were lined with inscriptions, Christian on one side, and heathen on the other.

Nothing can be more becoming than this modest approach, at every step growing in interest and value, towards the clustered temples of that acropolis or capitol of art. You walk along an avenue, one side adorned by the stately and mature or even decaying memorials of heathen dominion, the other by the young and growing and vigorous monuments of early Christian culture. There they stand face to face, as if in hostile array, about to begin a battle long since fought and won. On the right may be read the laudatory epitaphs of men whose families were conspicuous in republican Rome; long inscriptions descriptive of their victories, and commemorative of the titles, of Nerva or Trajan; then dedications to deities, announcements of their feasts, or fairs in their honour; and an endless variety of edicts, descriptions of property, sacred and domestic, and sepulchral monuments. The great business of a mighty empire, military, administrative, religious, and social, stands catalogued on that wall. What can ever take its place? And the outward form exhibits stability and high civilisation. These various records are inscribed with all the elegance of an accomplished stone-mason's chisel, in straight lines and in bold uncial letters; with the occasional ornaments and reliefs, that bespeak the sculptor; on blocks or slabs of valuable marbles, with an elegance of phrase that moves the scholar's envy.

Opposite to these imperial monuments are arranged a multitude of irregular, broken fragments of marble, picked up apparently here and there, on which are scratched, or crookedly carved, in a rude latinity and inaccurate orthography, short and simple notes, not living achievements, but of deaths and burials. There are no sounding titles, no beautiful pretensions. This is to a "sweet" wife, that to "a most innocent child," a third to "a well deserving" friend. If the other side records victories, this only speaks of losses; if that roars of wars, this murmurs only soft peace; if that adorns with military trophies, this illuminates with scourges and pincers: the one may perhaps surmount with the soaring eagle, the other crowns with the olive-bearing dove.

Here are two antagonist races, speaking in their monuments, like the front lines of two embattled armies, about to close in earnest and decisive battle: the strong one, that lived upon and over the earth, and thrust its rival beneath it, then slept secure like Jupiter above the buried Titans; and the weak and contemptible, that burrowed below, and dug its long deep mines, and enrolled its deaths in them, almost under the palaces whence issued decrees for its extermination, and the amphitheatres to which it was dragged up from its caverns to fight with wild beasts. At length the mines were sprung, and heathenism tottered, fell, and crashed, like Dagon, on its own pavements. And, through the rents and fissures, basilicas started up from their concealment below, cast in moulds of sand, unseen, in those depths; altar and chancel, roof and pavement, baptistery and pontifical chair, up they rose in brick and marble, wood or bronze, what they had been in friable sandstone below. A new empire, new laws; a new civilisation, a new art, a new learning, a new morality, covered the space occupied by the monuments to which the inscriptions opposite belonged.

It was a mercy to Christianity, that Providence kept the destruction of the previous state out of its deliberation, and in Its own hands. To have kept up its monuments would have been impossible. What could Christians have done with thermae, amphitheatres, and their lewd representations? Yet to have destroyed them would have been called barbarous. So God "lifted up a sign to the nations afar off, and whistled to them from the ends of the earth, and they came with speed swiftly."[1] "There came up water out of the north; there was an overflowing torrent; and they covered the land, and all that was therein; the city, and inhabitants thereof."[2] The successive locust-swarms that rushed over Italy had no instinct to guide them but the barbarism that plunders what it covets, and destroys what it contemns. And even after this, when the monuments of paganism had been destroyed, He "hissed for the fly that was in the uppermost part of the rivers of Egypt, and for the bee that was in

1. Holy Bible: Isaias: 5. 26.   2. Jeremias: 47. 2.

the land of Assyria; and they came, and they rested in the torrents of the valleys, and in the holes of the rocks."[1] For the Saracen predatory incursions in the eighth century devastated the outlying Christian monuments, and caused the final spoliation of the catacombs.

The Church has kindly taken into her keeping the gathered fragments and ruins of both invasions, from north and from east; and here they are placed separate, but united, and in peace. Thus you are prepared for that still higher evidence that the Church is neither Goth nor Vandal, which shines bright before you, in those precious halls and graceful cabinets, in which successive Popes, whose names they bear, have worthily, or daintily, preserved the treasures and gems of ancient art.

After his restoration, Pius VII continued his interrupted work. It is recorded of Fray Luis de Leon, the eminent Spanish professor, that, having been suspended from his chair for five years through hostile intrigue, and having been triumphantly restored, his lecture-room was crowded to hear, as it was hoped, his indignant vindication of himself. If they were disappointed, they were doubtless edified, when the audience heard him quietly commence by: "*Heri dicebamus,*" "In yesterday's lesson we were saying:" and continue the subject of his last lecture. It was with just such serenity that the good Pontiff calmly resumed the works of his glorious reign, "*Ibi manum apposuit ubi opus desiderat.*" [At that point he set his hand to the task which was required.] The gallery which more especially bears his name, and which crosses the great Belvedere court of the Vatican, is one of the most beautiful portions of the Museum. It seems indeed wonderful how such a building could have been erected, richly decorated, and filled with master-pieces of art, in so short a time. When I first remember it, it was still in the

1. Holy Bible: Isaias: 7. 18-19.

mason's hands, brick walls amidst a forest of scaffold poles; yet the Pope lived to see it finished in all its beauty. The architect, if I remember rightly, was not so fortunate. He was young and promising, with the north-ern name of Stern. I can recollect going to see him, at Monte Compatri, in the Tusculan hills, when he was disfigured by a huge tumour on his shoulder, the conse-quence of a fall, which shortly carried him to an early grave.

To the library Pius made considerable additions, not only of manuscripts, but of many thousands of printed vol-umes. Among these was a magnificent collection of Bibles, and biblical works. The Pantheon had long been to Rome, what Santa Croce was to Florence, and Westminster Abbey once was to us; the mausoleum of great men. The busts of distinguished Italians were ranged around its walls, and gave a profane appearance to the church. By order of the Sovereign Pontiff a new gallery was prepared in the Capitol, under the name of Protomotheca; and in one night of 1820, the whole of the busts were removed from the Pantheon, and carried thither.

It is, however, one even greater glory of Pius' reign, that he commenced that series of excavations round ancient monuments which have been continued till the present day, and have done more for solid antiquarian learning than any previous study. Former excavations had been carried on mainly to obtain works of art, and were filled up again as fast as made. But, in 1807, the arch of Septimus Severus, which, as may be seen in Piranesi's prints (not, here "the lying Piranesi," as Forsyth calls him), had been more than half buried in the ground, was cleared of all rubbish, and an open space left quite round it. An immense spur, too, was added to the Colosseum, to prevent a large portion of its outward wall falling. The excavations and restorations of ancient monuments were continued by the French authorities under the Empire, and often with a bolder

hand, for churches were destroyed or desecrated to discover or restore heathen edifices.[1] But after the restoration
the work was resumed with vigour. Archaeologists were
wonderfully disappointed, when on excavating round a column in the centre of the Forum, which had been the very
pivot of systems, it displayed on its pedestal an inscription
of Phocas, a monarch totally out of the pale of classical
society. Besides, however, other interesting restorations,
that of the arch of Titus reflects the greatest credit on the
commission appointed by Pius for the preservation of
ancient edifices. This, not only beautiful, but precious monument had, by the Frangipani family, been made the
nucleus of a hideous castellated fort. Its masonry, however,
embraced and held together, as well as crushed the marble
arch; so that on freeing it from its rude buttresses, there was
a fear of its collapsing; and it had first to be well bound
together by props and bracing beams, a process in which
Roman architects are unrivalled. It was in this condition
that I first remember the arch of Titus. The seven-branched

1. I remember reading in Dr. Heber's "Journal," that an Armenian
priest had called upon him, strong and powerful, and with a stentorian
voice, to ask a contribution towards the repairing of the church belonging to his nation and order in Rome, Santa Maria Egiziaca, anciently
the temple of Fortuna Virilis. The Anglican prelate refused him,
because he said he had never heard that the French damaged ancient
monuments, and he did not believe his story. The fact was, the Armenian and the Englishman looked at the thing from opposite points of
view. The former considered the destruction of modern additions, and
restitution of his church to heathen forms, a spoliation and an injury;
the latter considered it a benefit, probably. He was right in supposing
that the French would not destroy a pagan temple; but not, in believing
that they would spare a church. As a singular coincidence I may add
that, just after reading this passage when first published, I heard a very
loud voice in my ante-room, as Dr. Heber said he had heard one in his.
It struck me that it might be the very Armenian, and so it was. He was
astonished and amused at finding himself examined about his interview
at Calcutta. He confirmed the facts; but thought that the bishop had
treated him very shabbily.

candlestick, the table, the trumpets, and other spoils of the temple, which Reland has so well illustrated in a learned little treatise, as collateral and monumental evidence of Scripture truth, were invisible in great measure behind the wooden framework, which also completely hid from view the beautiful relief of the apotheosis in the key-stone. The simple expedient was adopted by the architect Stern of completing the arch in stone; for its sides had been removed. Thus encased in a solid structure, which continued all its architectural lines, and renewed its proportions to the mutilated centre, the arch was both completely secured, and almost restored to its pristine elegance.

CHAPTER X

BRIGANDAGE

I MIGHT be reproached for overlooking one of the most vivid though painful, recollections of youth, if nothing appeared in these pages on a subject which, at the period that occupies us, made impressions not easily effaced from memory. Indeed, by some who remember those times, it may be considered a blot upon them, and a proof of weakness in the ruler and his minister. At no time, indeed, were the rovers from the desert more daring, or their atrocities more dreadful, than after the restoration of the pontifical government. And yet, it would be most unjust to throw on that government the blame.

Let us begin by remarking that no one has ever charged the French government, which preceded that event, with feebleness or mistaken mercy. On the contrary, the code of repression was perfectly Draconian, and it was ruthlessly carried out. The slightest connivance at or abetting of brigandism was death, summarily inflicted. To be found with a small provision of food, was capitally punished in a shepherd who guarded a flock in the solitudes of the mountains. Hence, boys have been executed, with men that had dragged them within the snares of the law, although those that accompanied them to the scaffold have assured the writer that they were as innocent as infants of the crime of highway robbery. And hence, too, the poor shepherds were often in a fearful dilemma: if they saw the *banditti*, and did not denounce them, they suffered as abettors and accomplices; if they set the patrol on their track, they ran the risk of assassination. Sometimes a more cruel expedient was adopted. Many of that time will remember a poor peasant boy, who used to beg for alms in Rome, whose tongue had been barbarously cut out by the roots, that he might not be able to betray to the police the passage of a robber band.

If the intense severity of the French laws, and if the unceasing pursuit of well-disciplined troops, could not put down the peculiar form of robbery known in Italian by the terms of "*crassazione*" and "*assassinio*," and yet the government that employed these means unsuccessfully has never been taxed with feebleness, why should the one which immediately succeeded it be accused of that defect? Surely the causes which made brigandage indomitable before, could not have ceased or diminished after the restoration of the pontifical government. The pressure of a military rule, which did not even affect to have anything paternal about it, was removed; and the effective army which had garrisoned all the country was withdrawn. It was only to be expected that the lawless spirit of the forest and the crag would acquire hardihood and power. It was not, in fact, till both the police and soldiery had been thoroughly reorganised, that the evil was, through them, completely put down. This was only in the following pontificate.

The struggle, under such varied circumstances, between society and lawlessness, and the return of the latter to open war, after it had been repeatedly and effectually suppressed, are evidence of causes peculiar to the country, the absence of which forms security elsewhere. A mountainous country, for instance, will encourage a character of crime different from what will flourish in one like ours. A ridge of high mountains, almost inaccessible in parts, traversed only through deep and narrow ravines, commanded by over-hanging cliffs, with one state at its feet on one side and another on the other, forms a sort of "no man's land," the chosen abode of the outlaw. If a small knot is once formed there by a daring chief, who may possibly be a volunteer, having a dash of false romance in his character, and loving a mischievous vagabond life in preference to one of honest toil, it soons swells into a band, by successive adhesions of escaped or liberated convicts, runaways from pursuing jus-tice, or mere idle scapegraces, who gradually inure themselves to deeds of blood, and become elated to some-thing of military feeling by the terror which they inspire. Then they contrive, like Dick Turpin and others of our cel-ebrated highwaymen, to mingle in their acts of daring some instances of generous gallantry, or polite forbearance, or even charitable kindness, which gain them sympathy among neighbours, and a character of knight-errantry among tourists. All this is bad enough, for it gives to their combats with the representatives of order a colour of chivalrous warfare, instead of the darker hue of a felon's struggle with the ministers of justice.

But worse still are the obstacles to success against them, from their favoured position. By timely warnings from secret sharers in their booty, or depraved allies, they hear, or used to hear, in time, of the approach of any armed force against them; their own scouts, from "coigns of van-tage" on the cornice of a rocky battlement, or from tree-tops, gave notice of the immediate approach of dan-ger. Surprise was rendered almost impossible; and a scrambling attack through ravines, up rugged crags, and amidst tangled brushwood, had, to regular troops from the plain, all the disadvantages and perils, without its dignity, of a guerilla combat. It cannot be denied that the conduct of the soldiers was intrepid and worthy of a better battle-field; but often when they had forced the position of a robber band, it would spring over the boundary line of another state, and there defy its baffled pursuers. This was something like the security in London, not very long ago, of delinquents and *gamins*, if they could get through Temple Bar, and thus take a serene view of the white-badged pursuivant, who stood foiled on the other side. In both cases, it was not till the convention was made between Rome and Westminster of the one side, and Naples and the City on the other side, that the police of the one might pass the boundaries of the other in pursuit of lawful game, that the robbers began to have the worst of it. The agreement between the two Italian powers took place in 1818, but proved insufficient. What was necessary and was resorted to later was contemporary cooperation from both sides; a sort of tiger-hunt, in which the whole jungle is netted round and the quarry hemmed in, so that no pursuit is necessary because no flight is possible.

If the reader wishes to refresh his memory on the exploits of the *banditti* of that period, and recall their practices and mode of life, he has only to turn to Washington Irving's *Tales of a Traveller*, where, in the third part, he gives "The Painter's Adventure" among his robber stories. In his preface he says that "the Adventure of the Young Painter" among the *banditti* is taken almost entirely from an authentic narrative in manuscript." True: and astonished and disappointed was the poor French artist, when he found that the manuscript which he used to lend freely to his friends had been translated and published without his permission or knowledge by M. Wassington, as he called his literary pirate. The writer had read it as a work of fiction by the amusing American tourist; for who believes the account in prefaces, of manuscripts, whether found in a *Cura's* leather trunk, or "Old Mortality's wallet," or "Master Humphry's clock," or nowhere in particular? There was a contradiction, indeed, in calling that the adventure of a *young* painter, in which the author attributed his coolness and serenity among the robbers, to his having been "schooled to hardship during the late revolutions," that is, at the end of the last century. This might even be passed over but it was too true for M. Chatillon, the artist, that he had passed into the stage of the "lean and slippered pantaloon," when he was taken, as he describes, from the Villa Ruffinella, in 1818, by brigands, in mistake for its owner, Prince Lucien Bonaparte. The band had seized the chaplain as he strolled in the neighbouring woods before dinner, and detained him till dusk, when they compelled him to be their guide to the house.

M. Chatillon lent his manuscript, among other neighbours, to us of the English College; and I believe we were the first to discover and inform him, that it was already published in English, with such alterations as made the account apocryphal; but with such a charm as would deprive the original, if printed, of all chance of success. A few years ago, after his adventure, M. Chatillon became an intimate of Lord Shrewsbury's family, where he painted many portraits of friends, likenesses, but not pictures: and the reader of that melancholy book of the day, "*The Catalogue of Alton Towers*," will find the name of the "young painter," M. Chatillon, appended as the label to some very moderate works of art.

Washington Irving alludes to the carrying off of what he calls "the school of Terracina." It was in fact the episcopal seminary, situated outside the city, that was invaded one night; and all its inmates were carried away,—superiors, prefects, scholars and servants. On the road the brigands were intrepidly attacked by a single dragoon, named, I think, Ercoli, or Ercolani, who lost his life in the unequal contest. But it enabled some of the captives to escape and give the alarm. Others got away; the feeble were dimissed; till at last a few boys of the best families were alone retained in the mountain fastnesses. Letters were sent to their families, demanding sums of money for their ransom; the demand was complied with. The scouts of the robbers saw the bearers of it winding up the rocky path, mistook them for soldiers, and gave the alarm to the troop, saying they were betrayed. When the relations of the captives reached the summit, they found two or three innocent children strapped to trees, with their throats cut, and dead. The survivors were brought to Rome, to tell their sad tale to the good and tender-hearted Pius; and well the writer remembers seeing the poor boys still under the influence of their terror. They were retained at Rome.

But the recollections of that period furnish another event, which earlier than this, brought nearer home the anxieties of country life, even when passed in community. The English College possesses a country-house, deliciously situated in the village of Monte Porzio. Like most villages in the Tusculan territory, this crowns a knoll, which in this instance looks as if it had been kneaded up from the valleys beneath it; so round, so shapely, so richly bosoming does it swell upwards; and so luxuriously clothed is it with the three gifts whereby "men are multiplied,"[1] that the village and its church seem not to sit on a rocky summit, but to be half sunk into the lap of the olive, the vine, and the waving corn, that reach the very houses. While the entrance and front of this villa are upon the regular streets of the little town, the garden side stands upon the very verge of the hilltop; and the view, after plunging at once to the depths of the valley, along which runs a shady road, rises up a gentle acclivity, vine and olive clad; above, this is clasped by a belt of stately chestnuts, the bread-tree of the Italian peasant; and thence springs a round craggy mound, looking stern and defiant like what it was—the citadel of Tusculum. Upon its rocky front our students have planted a huge cross.

Such is the view which presents itself immediately opposite the spectator, if leaning over the low parapet of the English garden. The beauties to right and to left

1. Holy Bible: Psalm: 4.8.

belong not to our present matter. Well, just where the
vineyards touch the woods, as if to adorn both, there lies
nestling what you would take to be a very neat regular village. A row of houses, equidistant and symmetrical, united
by a continuous dwarf wall, and a church with its towers in
the midst, all of dazzling whiteness, offer no other sugges-
tion. The sight certainly would deceive one; but not so the
ears. There is a bell that knows no sleeping. The peasant
hears it as he rises at day-break to proceed to his early toil,
the vine-dresser may direct every pause for refreshment by
its unfailing regularity through the day; the horseman
returning home at evening uncovers himself as it rings
forth the "Ave;" and the muleteer singing on the first of
his string of mules, carrying wine to Rome, is glad at mid-
night to catch its solemn peal as it mingles with the tinkle
of his own drowsy bells. Such an unceasing call to prayer
and praise can be answered not by monks nor by friars, but
only by anchorites.

And to such does this sweet abode belong. A nearer
approach does not belie the distant aspect. It is as neat, as
regular, as clean, and as tranquil as it looks. It is truly a village divided by streets, in each of which are rows of houses
exactly symmetrical. A small sitting-room, a sleeping cell, a
chapel completely fitted up, in case of illness, and a wood
and lumber-room, compose the cottage. This is approached
by a garden, which the occupant tills, but only for flowers,
assisted by his own fountain abundantly supplied. While
singing None in choir, the day's only meal is deposited in a
little locker within the door of the cell, for each one's solitary refection. On a few great festivals they dine together;
but not even the Pope, at his frequent visits, has meat
placed before him. Everything, as has been said, is scrupu-
lously clean. The houses, inside and out, the well-furnished
library, the strangers' apartments (for hospitality is freely
given), and still more the church, are faultless in this
respect. And so are the venerable men who stand in choir,
and whose noble voices sustain the church's magnificent

psalmody, with unwavering slowness of intonation. They are clad in white from head to foot; their thick woollen drapery falling in large folds; and the shaven head, but flowing beard, the calm features, the downcast eyes, and often venerable aspect, make every one a picture, as solemn as Zurbaran ever painted, but without the sternness which he sometimes imparts to his recluses. They pass out of the church, to return home, all silent and unnoticing; but the guest-master will tell you who they are. I remember but a few. There is a native of Turin, who was a general in Napoleon's army, fought many battles, and has hung up his sword beside the altar, to take down in its place the sword of the spirit, and fight the good fight within. The next is an eminent musician, who has discovered the hollowness of human applause, and has unstrung his earthly harp, and taken up "the lyre of the Levite," to join his strains to those of angels. Another comes "curved like a bride's arch," as Dante says, and leaning on a younger arm, as he totters forward; one whose years are ninety, of which seventy have been spent in seclusion, except a few of dispersion, but in peace: for he refuses any relaxation from his duties. Then follows a fourth, belonging to one of the noblest Roman families, who yet prefers his cottage and his lentil to the palace and the banquet.

Such was the Camaldoli, and such were its inmates, when a robber chief determined to carry them off into the mountains. The gardens, woods, and fields of the hermit-village were all enclosed with a high wall, except where the gardens looked into the valley which separated it from Monte Porzio. Over one of these walls, intended for seclusion not defence, the wolf climbed into the peaceful fold. One by one the unsuspecting inmates were aroused from their slumber to unholy Matins; and soon found themselves assembled in front of the church, surrounded by a large band of ruffians, armed to the teeth, muttering curses and blasphemies to smother their remorse. It was the policy of these wretches to leave not one behind who might betray

their deed; and all were commanded to march out of the
gate, and take the steep path towards Tusculum.

Remonstrance seemed vain; there was but one sturdy
lad, a farm-servant, not in the habit, who might have
escaped, but would not. He had been there from boyhood,
and loved the good hermits as his parents. He bodly
argued with the marauders; he checked and reproved
them; he insisted on the old, old men, and the infirm,
being left behind; he made such hasty preparations of food
as time permitted; he soothed and encouraged the more
timid, and went forth with them. On the journey, he was a
hand to the weak, and a foot to the weary; and feared not
to expostulate with the freebooters.

Next morning, the early bell was silent; it was the clock
of the neighbourhood, so the silence was ominous and
inconvenient. Hour after hour went by;—was there no
chaunt, no oblation, no sacred duty at Camaldoli? One
may easily imagine the horror and consternation spread
on every side, as the news travelled round, of the sacrile-
gious abduction of these unoffending, most respected, and
most charitable men; from whose gate no poor man was
ever known to depart unrelieved. The history was related
by the two or three left, through necessity, behind, and by
those who gradually escaped during the several days'
march, or were allowed to return, as obstacles to rapid
movements soon required.

A large ransom was demanded for the few retained as
hostages. It was the Government that was expected to pay
it. A strong detachment of soldiers was sent instead. It
overtook the brigands unprepared; volleys were fired on
both sides, and in the affray all the religious escaped except
one. A musket ball had broken his thigh, and he lay help-
less on the ground. But the robbers were worsted, and he
was saved. He belonged to the noble family of Altemps,
whose palace, opposite the church of Sant' Apollinare, was
designed or decorated by Baldassare Peruzzi, and contains
an apartment intact since it was occupied by St. Charles

Borromeo. To this family residence he was conveyed, and there was attended for a long time, till at length cured. He was offered leave to retire from the monastic state, and remain as a priest in the world; but he declined, and returned, though to another Camaldoli.

To the sight and to the ears, our Tusculum hermitage underwent a change. The fold required better guarding. The low walls between the gardens on our side, were built up to a formidable height, and slashed with rows of loop-holes, so as to be defensible by the fire-arms of secular servants. The beautiful prospect of the valley and the campagna beyond was shut up to the tenants of the border cottages; the square bit of the heavens over their gardens was all now left them. While we would see this change we could hear another. The deep bay of enormous and fierce ban-dogs echoed through the night, more unceasing than the bell. They were kept chained up all day; at night they were let loose, and woe to any one who should have presumed to approach them without the Camaldolese habit. It was the only thing they respected. The faithful servant put it on; and often have I seen him, and spoken to him of his robber adventure, while he discharged, as an edifying lay brother, the duties of porter.

It will be easily imagined how this daring attack upon aged and poor religious was calculated to awaken some uneasiness in a smaller ecclesiastical body, only separated by a narrow valley, and occupying a corresponding situation opposite; and moreover having the fatal reputation of being rich, and of belonging to a nation of fabulous wealth. This occurrence certainly brought the idea of danger nearer home; but there had been an occurrence which had brought it nearer self.

On the 16th of October, 1819, being, for the first time, in the enjoyment of the delights of the *villeggiatura* in our country-house, we made, in a considerable body, our first visit to the ruins of Tusculum. Our worthy rector was there, and of the party was the Professor of Ecclesiastical

History of the Roman College, afterwards Cardinal Ostini. We were immersed in the pit of the little Roman theatre, and entangled in the brambles and underwood that now cushion its seats, when suddenly there came upon the stage a party of most unexpected actors. About eighteen or twenty men made their appearance, as though they had sprung from some secret trap, or from a cavern in the wood around us. Whether purposely, or accidentally, they hemmed us in, standing above the party. The looks of terror imprinted on the countenances of one or two of our body are not easily to be forgotten.

The men had most of the external attributes by which *banditti* are to be recognised on and off the stage; conical hats with hawks' feathers stuck in them, jackets, leggings or sandals, gay sashes, and carbines, carried, not on the back, but in the hand, with a jaunty ease that showed an amiable readiness to let them off. Every one tried to get as far away as possible; the writer was dragging through the bushes a spitefully restive *cavalcatura*,[1] and remained last.

"Are you from the English College?" asked the chief, with a stern countenance. "No," cried out one of the strangers in our party. Now our very accent would have betrayed us, if deceit could have been thought of, even to *banditti*.

"Yes," was the reply, from a quarter still nearer. Each rejoinder was true in the mouth of the speaker. "How many are you?" "Ten." This seemed still more ominous. But the next question scarcely left room for hope. "Have you seen the armed patrol of Frascati anywhere about?" A gasping "No" was the necessary answer. A pause of a few moments ensued. "Speak civilly to them," some one said, much in the way Morton advised; "Speak them, fair, sirs; speak them fair," when treating with Claverhouse's dragoons. But it was unnecessary. The pause was broken by the captain, saying civilly enough, "*Buon giorno*," and leading off his troop.

1. a mount; it is unclear what kind of animal Wiseman had been riding.

The step from the sublime of terror to the ridiculous of courage was instantaneous. Of course no one had been frightened, and nobody had taken them for robbers. They were probably the patrol from some neighbouring village; for each was obliged to arm its youth, and scour the neighbouring woods. However, one had the opportunity of experiencing the feelings incident to falling among robbers with real fire-arms and imaginary fierce looks.

If this topic has been made prominent among the recollections of a memorable period, it is to show the desire to speak impartially, and not to conceal blots. That immense energy was displayed by the Government to efface them, and great sacrifices were made, no one who recollects the period can fail to remember. Military law reigned in the infested districts, to this extent, that the principal *banditti* were condemned to death as outlaws, and their sentence published with descriptions of their persons: so that nothing more was required, when they were taken, than to identify their persons, and proceed to the execution of the sentence. This was frequently done; and prices set upon their heads secured them to justice, if they descended from their haunts. It was proposed even to remove the inhabitants of districts that appeared incurable. Impunity was offered to such as delivered themselves up, on conditions somewhat analogous to our tickets of leave; and men used to be pointed out in Rome who had once been bandits, but were then leading a peaceful and industrious life.

But there was evidently a moral obstacle to the eradication of this dreadful system of outlaw life. It becomes habitual to families and to tracts of country; where its horrors, its cruelties, and its wickedness are almost forgotten in the recklessness and dashing exploits, the sure and enormous gains, and the very hair-breadth escapes that attend it. Hot blood easily leads to offence against the person; and one such crime drives its author to seek impunity, by war against the society that would justly punish him.

Let us, however, be always just. This great curse of Italy is impossible with us: we have no chains of Apennines, no rocky fastnesses, no mountain forests. But surely there have been lately here sufficient crimes, dark and cold, reaching to shedding of blood and to the heedless ruin of thousands, which may be reduced to classes, and are traceable to social and local diseases, from which Italy is exempt.

One further remark. Within these few years a system somewhat similar to that already detailed has revived; but more in the northern provinces. Again it is the fruit of a disturbance of public order, by revolution instead of by war. Again its seat is a border district, where the mountain boundary line is traced between Tuscany and the Papal States. And again this consequence of an abnormal condition is imputed to the normal; the legitimate sovereign is held responsible for the evils resulting from rebellion against him; and they who write to stimulate revolution, use as an argument in its favour, the necessity of repressing a mischief which revolution has engendered.

CHAPTER XI

CLOSE OF PIUS THE SEVENTH'S PONTIFICATE

THE venerable Pope had nearly reached the years of Peter, which none of his predecessors had yet attained; though sincere is the hope in the hearts of many of us, that the charm may be broken by the ninth Pius. Twenty-four years is the term thus assigned, as the bourn which none may hope to pass; and Pius VII had happily advanced far into his twenty-third. The sixth of July was the fourteenth anniversary of his seizure in the Quirinal palace by General Radet. On that day, in the year 1823, in the same place, the aged Pontiff, about six in the evening, being alone, rose from his chair, and leaning with one hand on the bureau before it, sought with the

other a cord balustrade which went around his room. He
missed it; his foot slipped, and he fell. He cried for help;
his attendants rushed in and laid him on his bed. He com-
plained of acute pain in his left side, and as soon as
surgical aid was procured it was discovered that the neck
of the femur was fractured—the very accident which had
so lately befallen Radetzky.

For eight days the Pope was kept in ignorance of the
gravity of his condition. When informed of it, he received
the news with the serenity and fortitude which had distinguished him in the vicissitudes of his life. He lingered for
six weeks, the object of affectionate solicitude to all Rome.
A person intimately connected with our college was in the
Pope's household, and brought us daily information of every
variation in his health.

It was while in this state of anxiety, that all Rome was
startled one morning by news so melancholy, and so naturally connected with the august patient, that in ancient
times it would have been considered a portent, beyond statues sweating blood in the Forum, or victims speaking in the
temples. It was rumoured that the great basilica of St. Paul's
beyond the walls was burnt down, and was already only a
heap of smoking ruins.

It was too true, though it seemed hard to conceive how it
was possible. The walls were of massive bricks, the pillars of
matchless Phrygian marble in the central, and of inferior marble in the lateral aisles, for it was a five-aisled church. There
were no flues or fires at any time, let alone the dog-days. Like
Achilles, these old churches have their one vulnerable point,
though its situation is reversed. The open cedar roof, sodden
dry, and scorched to a cinder, through ages of exposure, under
a scanty tiling, to a burning sun, forms an unresisting prey to
the destructive wantonness of a single spark. It was the usual
story; plumbers had been working on that roof, and had left a
pan of coals upon one of the beams. Every sort of rumour was,
however, started and believed. It was confidently reported to
be the work of incendiaries, and part of an atrocious plan to

destroy the sacred monuments of Rome.

It was not till the afternoon that either the heat of the season or the occupations of the day permitted one to go far beyond the gates, though the sad news had penetrated into every nook of the city at sunrise. Melancholy indeed was the scene. The tottering external walls were all that was permitted to be seen, even from a respectful distance; for it was impossible to know how long they would stand. A clear space was therefore kept around, in which the skilful and intrepid fire-brigade—an admirably organised body—were using all their appliances to prevent the flames breaking out from the smouldering ruins.

There, among others, was the enthusiastic Avvocato Fea, almost frantic with grief. He was not merely an antiquarian in sculptures and inscriptions, he was deeply versed in ecclesiastical history, and loved most dearly its monuments. St. Paul's was one of the most venerable and most precious of these. The very abandonment of the huge pile, standing in solitary grandeur on the banks of the Tiber, was one source of its value. While it had been kept in perfect repair, little or nothing had been done to modernise it and alter its primitive form and ornaments, excepting the later additions of some modern chapels above the transept; it stood naked and almost rude, but unencumbered with the lumpish and tasteless plaster, and encasement of the old basilica in a modern Berninesque church, which had disfigured the Lateran cathedral under the pretence of supporting it.

It remained genuine, though bare, as St. Apollinaris in Classe at Ravenna,—the city eminently, of unspoiled basilicas. No chapels, altars or mural monuments softened the severity of its outlines; only the series of papal portraits, running round the upper lines of the walls, redeemed this sternness. But the unbroken files of columns, along each side, carried the eye forward to the great central object, the altar and its "Confession;" while the secondary rows of pillars running behind the principal ones, gave depth and shadow, mass and solidity, to back up the noble avenue along which one glanced.

Among the constant and bewildered cries of Fea was: "Save the triumphal arch!" He made light now apparently of the rest. The term is applied to the great arch, which, supported on two massive pillars, closes the nave, or rather separates it from the transept and apse beyond. Above this arch rises a wall, clothed in mosaic, now happily revived and perfected, of the Theodosian period. The triumphal arch of St. Paul's still towered nobly among the ruins, almost unscathed, as did the Gothic ciborium or marble canopy over the altar. On the face of the arch remained the majestic figure of our Lord in glory; and round it a metrical inscription, in which the Empress Galla Placida recounted how, assisted by the great Pontiff Leo, she had finished the decorations of the church built by preceeding emperors.

This mosaic was, in some sort, the very title-deed of the modern church, its evidence of identity with the imperial basilica. To preserve it just where it had stood for 1400 years would be almost to annul the effects of the conflagration; it would make the new edifice a continuation of the old.

This was attended to. One of the first steps taken was carefully to remove all that remained of the ancient mosaic, by the skilful hands of the Vatican workmen in that exquisite art; and one of the last was to restore it to its place over the rebuilt arch.

To return, not a word was spoken to the sick Pontiff on this dreadful calamity. At St. Paul's he had lived as a quiet monk, engaged in study and in teaching, and he loved the place with the force of an early attachment. It would have added a mental pang to his bodily sufferings, to learn the total destruction of that venerable sanctuary, in which he had drawn down, by prayer, the blessings of heaven on his youthful labour.

In this happy ignorance the revered patient lingered on. To reunite the fractured bone, at his age, was beyond the power of surgery; his feebleness increased, and he seemed to be slowly sinking; when, on the 16th of August, more active symptoms supervened, especially delirium. On the following day, the Holy Pontiff expressed his desire to receive the Viaticum, and it was administered to him by Cardinal Bertazzoli. Thus strengthened with the Bread of Angels, he awaited calmly his end. On the nineteenth he received Extreme Unction, and orders were sent to all churches to recite in every Mass, the prayer "for the Pontiff at the point of death." While it was being said all through Rome, on the following morning, the venerable man closed his glorious pontificate, and fell asleep in the Lord.

Providence had given him in the latter years of his pontificate many soothing and cheering compensations. In 1819 the Emperor and Empress of Austria, with their daughter, visited Rome, attended by a numerous and brilliant suite. It was not an *incognito* affair: they came in their own imperial character; and right imperially were they received and treated. Without disturbing the Pope or his court, a splendid suite of apartments was prepared for the imperial party in the Quirinal Palace, and furnished in a style which strongly contrasted with the severity of pontifical dwellings. Among the recollections of the period, there rise, distinct and vivid, the public *fêtes* given in honour of these illustrious guests.

The King of Prussia visited Rome in 1822 in a more private manner, and afforded us an opportunity to see the Nestor of science, Humboldt. But in Rome, at that time, one became familiar with royal lineaments.

The King of Naples visited in 1821. King Charles IV of Spain and his Queen had chosen Rome for their abode: in 1819 he went to Naples, to recruit his health, and there died, while she remained at home, sickened too and died. Neither ever learnt any news, on this side of the grave, of the other's illness or death.

Charles Emmanuel IV of Savoy had also retired to Rome, old and blind. I can well remember seeing him kneeling before the altar of Santa Maria Maggiore on Christmas Day, feeble and supported by two attendants. This was on my first Christmas in Rome: he died the following year. Our own banished Queen sought refuge there for a time;[1] and it must have been a consolation to the meek and unresentful Pius to see his capital afford a shelter to the proscribed family of the Emperor from whom he had so much suffered. They were allowed to have their palaces, their estates, their titles, and their position, not only unmolested, but fully recognised. And no one surely lived more respected, or died more regretted than the Princess Laetitia, the Emperor's honoured mother. This is truly a noble prerogative of Rome, to be the neutral territory on which the representatives of rival and even hostile houses may meet in peace, and with dignity; a place where enmities are forgotten, and injuries buried in oblivion.

And, in the same manner, one who resides in Rome may hope to see many men celebrated for their genius or their industry, in every department of literature and science, as well as art. Several of these have been mentioned, to whom others might be added, either residents in Rome, or passing visitors of its treasures.

But far beyond all these extraneous glories, which shed an ennobling splendour round the old age and waning pontificate of Pius VII was the steady and unvarying love and veneration of his subjects. Not a murmur jarred upon his ear, among the benedictions daily wished him, and returned by him with fatherly tenderness to all. One may doubt if there be an instance in history, where the judgment of posterity is less likely to reverse the verdict of contemporaries.

---

1. Caroline of Brunswick, the estranged wife of George IV who was never crowned Queen. While in Rome, a speech is attributed to her, which even those who will not consider it irreverent, will think undignified. She there heard that her name had been struck out of prayers in the national liturgy, and remarked: "They have prayed a long time for me as Princess of Wales, and I am no better for it; perhaps now that they have given up praying for me, I may improve." MS *Journal*.

§ INDEX §

Most recent books
THE CARDINAL'S SNUFF-BOX
A villa in the Italian lake district, in a summer of the late 1890s; a castle in a garden, a lake, and snow-capped mountains in the distance; a beautiful woman glimpsed a few times in the past; a young aspiring novelist.
In this elegant novel Henry Harland has combined an amusing and observant narrative with an exploration of opposing religious and philosophical views of life, which are ultimately reconciled by a pig, a storm, and a cardinal with the help of his snuff-box.
170 pages   £8.99

PILGRIMS TO JERUSALEM
Selection of personal accounts of pilgrimages to the Holy Places during the last 2,000 years. Editor, Antony Matthew, provides a chronology and extensive historical background on relations between Christianity, Islam and Judaeism
336 pages   *with illustrations by Mary Tyler*   £12.99

SET THE ECHOES FLYING
AN ANTHOLOGY OF POEMS, SONGS AND HYMNS
The 260 items include most of the favourites of England, Ireland, Scotland, and Wales. 500 years of great work to inspire, amuse and comfort. A bedside book for all ages.
272 pages   *with illustrations by Mary Tyler*   £10.99
Other titles
Robert Hugh Benson: Confessions of a Convert	£5.99
Elizabeth Butler—Battle Painter: Autobiography	£7.99
G K Chesterton: Autobiography (2nd edition)	£11.99
G.K. Chesterton: A Short History of England	£9.99
William Cobbett: A History of the Protestant Reformation	£9.99
F Marion Crawford: The Heart of Rome (novel)	£7.99
Hugh Dormer DSO : War Diary	£7.99
Bernard Holland: Memoir of Kenelm Digby	£6.99
Helen Jackson: Ramona (novel)	£8.99
Antony Matthew: Pearl of Great Price	£5.95
John Henry Newman: Collected Poems	£8.99
Coventry Patmore: The Bow set in the Cloud (his best critical writings)	£8.99
Francis Thompson: Collected Poems	£9.99

If you have difficulty in getting Fisher Press books you can purchase them direct from Fisher Press, Post Office Box 42, Sevenoaks, Kent, England TN 15 6YN.

Telephone /Fax 01732 761830